MY LIFE AS A BIRDER

Vol. 2

A Collection of Stories

from Antarctica to Zululand

HARRIET DAVIDSON

CONTENTS

PROLOGUE:
HOW I BECAME A "BIRD-WATCHER"

I don't remember where I heard about the Audubon Camp of Wisconsin; probably from an article in the *National Audubon* magazine, to which we subscribed after birding friends beguiled us into joining the group of local bird-watchers. "Birders" had not yet become a common term.

With my eight- and nine-year-olds off to summer camps in 1955, freedom beckoned. I could drop the campers off in northern Michigan, then with my five-year-old as a companion, take the ferry across Lake Michigan and drive on to St. Paul, Minnesota, where my sister eagerly awaited my daughter's visit. After that, the short distance to Hunt Hill was an easy drive.

My first memory of the Audubon Camp of Wisconsin was embarrassment at not bringing binoculars. I didn't own a pair. Luckily, the Bushnell company had donated several pairs of very good optics for just such occasions.

My second memory was of standing in a tent to be shared, again luckily, by several high school science teachers who were there to earn credits toward advanced degrees. At a persistently loud bird call from the encircling forest, I blurted out, "What is that?!" In unison my experienced friends answered, "A *red-eyed vireo.*" My first new bird!

Every morning, nineteen-year-old Sandy Sprunt led a pre-breakfast bird walk. Each day's goal was to identify one hundred species. My five-foot-four person scrambled after long-legged Sandy's stride, fascinated at his expertise. Each afternoon a question on bird identification was posted on the bulletin board, and that always sent me to various bird guides for answers. I think I am the one who should have earned a degree. The memory of the *bittern's* throaty *"oonk-a-lunk"* in the marsh at dusk was among my fondest memories after my return home to Michigan. I had a head start on my birding career, but it was only a start.

In the fall of 1959, my husband and I, now owners of afford-able binoculars purchased from Sears & Roebuck, joined Will Russell and Davis Finch on their first expedition into northeast Canada and its offshore islands. Again I was amazed, not only at the expertise, but the enthusiasm of our young guides.

We had been promised sightings of ten new birds. Natu-rally, off Deer and Brier Islands the majority were seabirds. I have often relived the morning when, braced against a shelter-ing lighthouse wall, the whipping wind and tumultuous waves brought us a *Manx shearwater* fluttering low against the storm.

Another bright moment, on our last stop on Monhegan Island, was finding a little *pink-breasted flycatcher* perched on the edge of a cottage roof. I ran uphill nearly a half mile to find our leaders and announced that I "thought" I had found a *Say's phoebe,* which sent Davis flying down the mountainside to verify my identification. What was a western *flycatcher* doing on an Atlantic Ocean island?

Later a terrifying moment occurred when off Monhegan

Island a finback whale rose up under our small boat, bumped it gently, then submerged and swam away.

Thirteen years later, in January 1972, we were off on a birding tour of Mexico. Again our leaders were young and enthusiastic. Peter Alden and Chris Leahy led a small group of birders beginning on the coast of Mazatlán, through Tepic, San Blas, Valle de Bravo, Puebla, and Orizaba, to the oceanside of Veracruz and Palenque.

This time we were thrown into a cauldron of new nomenclatures. For example: *macaw, toucanet, cotinga, saltator, honeycreeper,* and *flowerpiercer.* We were grateful to find so many colorful birds so close to our own country.

It was at that moment, as I stared unbelievingly at my list of 222 new birds, that an interesting hobby exploded into a passion. The whole world was full of birds, and I, with my equally enthusiastic husband, set out to find them.

Here I offer my stories.

PART I
BIRD CHASES

NEW YEAR'S EVE ON ELLIOTT KEY
December 1982

B
ob, as we early on learned to call him, owner and captain of a sixteen-foot outboard motorboat, held out his arm to support me as I jumped over the gunwale and sat down on a forward thwart. Within minutes we were speeding over the choppy waters in Biscayne Bay, Florida, on our way to Elliott Key to search for a *La Sagra's flycatcher*, a totally drab little bird, which had flown out of the range of his home in the Bahamas, gotten lost, and now was hiding somewhere on the scrubby island. I mean really hiding. Five birders, who had been fruitlessly walking back and forth for two days, playing a recorded tape of the *flycatcher*'s two-note call, were waiting at the dock for a ride back to the mainland. It was noon and hot. In spite of the disappointing news, we paraded along the well-worn path that bisected the small island, until late in the afternoon, when our boatman returned to pick us up. We were too late. The bird was gone. As we departed for the airport in Miami, my husband handed Bob his business card, saying, "Keep in touch." It was the day after Christmas.

Three days later came a phone message from Bob. The *La Sagra's flycatcher* was again being seen on Elliott Key. He offered to meet our plane and transport us to the island. It was holiday time, but the next morning we set out for the airport carrying a well-worn navy seabag filled with two sleeping bags and a lightweight mountain tent, and we were on our way.

At the dockside deli, we purchased a dozen cheese-filled bagels (food that would not need refrigeration) and a few canned items. In spite of small-craft warnings, our small outboard lurched against the oncoming breakers until we bounced up and down like rubber balls, often landing severely on our tailbones. We were relieved to arrive safely near a small county park, which offered tables, benches, and a restroom for the convenience of picnickers and small boaters. We set up camp and began our search for the *flycatcher*.

Though we walked about all afternoon, no familiar two-note call was heard. A few other birders, sacrificing holiday time to go birding, arrived, became disheartened, and left. But one old friend remained: Thompson Marsh, an eighty-year-old University of Colorado law professor, who approached and timidly asked us if we possibly had enough food for him to stay overnight. He would sleep on a picnic bench and use his thin topcoat as a blanket. We agreed to stretch out our meager supplies of canned spaghetti and applesauce. Of course he could stay.

New Year's Eve began quietly with bagels for breakfast, then again the monotonous trudging along the now too-familiar path. Small sailboats and cruisers, crowded with noisy celebrants, began to assemble in the harbor. Then, in midmorning, it happened! The two-note call was so near we had only to crash through a few scraggly bushes into a small clearing, where we found the *La Sagra's flycatcher* calmly perched on a branch barely above our heads. Thompson was not far behind. Because he was so hard of hearing, he had remained near me all morning. I pulled him into the open space below the *flycatcher*. As he looked up at the little bird, the subject of so many hours of mingled hope and frustration, the success of our search brought a glowing smile to his face.

Other birders arrived — lucky guys to find the little lost bird so easily. But that happens. Bob sailed in for his return passengers, including our old overnight friend, who would get home just in time for Monday morning classes. We, with our heavy gear, would have to wait until the next day.

As darkness fell, disco music erupted from the harbor. Colorful Chinese lanterns, strung from ship to ship, formed a background for the dancing figures on shore. Rockets exploded, bursting into the night sky, fracturing into rainbow sprays. "Happy New Year!" shouted the revelers.

We dined on the last of the cheese-filled bagels, and chocolate-covered doughnuts donated by a departing friend earlier in the afternoon. Near dawn, the noise from the revelers began to recede and we finally fell asleep.

This had been a fine New Year's Eve celebration. A successful bird chase had ended the old year, and we had wonderful memories to begin the new one.

But as we returned to the mainland and civilization, I knew it would be years before I would eat another cheese-filled bagel!

THE SIBERIAN TIT: A RARE FIND
July 1985

iberian tits dwell in Siberia, don't they? That is why they are called *Siberian tits*, although in North America they have been renamed *gray-capped chickadees*. Probably right now there are lots of them fluttering among the dwarf willows at the edge of the Arctic Ocean as they glean their daily intake of insects.

So why am I looking for a *Siberian tit* in North America? Because I have heard that there are records of small flocks of the species breeding in Alaska and northern Canada. But where to look in that vast expanse of tundra-filled wilderness?

Then, one day in conversation with Will Russell, he described his encounter with the *tits* on a float trip down Alaska's Susitna River as his group camped at the confluence with the Kelly River. A year went by, but my desire to go after those birds persisted. Finally, after a few phone calls, the last one to the Baker Aviation office in Kotzebue, Alaska, a genial voice assured me that he, the pilot, was very familiar with the area as he made daily trips to drop supplies to nearby mining camps.

He flew a six-seater Cessna and would be happy to fly me and as many as four other passengers, the remaining space to be reserved for our camping cargo.

Right then I signed up for myself and my husband and immediately invited Gordon and Peggy Tans and Stacey Scott, Anchorage residents and dedicated birders, who eagerly accepted.

My husband and I flew into Anchorage on a lovely July day. Peggy and I went shopping for instant oatmeal for breakfasts, bread and sandwich makings, instant soup, and at the last minute we added a panful of Peggy's homemade coffee cake, a big bucket of Kentucky Fried Chicken for our first night's dinner in camp, and at the very last, a bag of oranges, after deciding that the extra weight was worth having the fresh fruit. We were ready to go.

True to his word, on Friday at noon our pilot softly landed us on the Kelly Bar, a broad expanse of alluvial sand. Dwarf willow bushes edged the two rivers, and a few minutes' walk would bring us to the edge of a dark pine forest. We stumbled from the little plane and drew in deep breaths of wonderful, clear, bracing air. The sun was shining. It was a perfect day, and we all agreed to immediately start our search. Setting up camp could wait.

Before entering the forest, my husband passed out police whistles, both as a safety measure and as a warning signal if one of us should encounter the bird. One blast would mean "We're lost; where are you?" but three blasts would mean "Come quick; bird in sight!"

We had taped a *National Geographic* recording of the *Siberian tit*'s high-pitched *"dear, dear, dear,"* and off we started, treading carefully atop the spongy moss and outbreaks of broken rocks from an ancient glacial age, expecting momentarily to hear an answer. The soft, burring call of the *boreal chickadees* became familiar. Eventually, tired from the long day of preparation and travel, we returned to our campsite, gathered wood from the abundant supply of driftwood along the shore, and built a roaring fire. Wind-felled logs became dining room chairs as we encircled the blaze and devoured our chicken dinner. Sleep came quickly in our lightweight mountain tents.

Saturday found us well rested, well fed, and exuberant. A whole day lay ahead of us to cover miles of the birds' territory. When the uncooperative *tits* did not appear during the morning hours, we inflated the rubber raft we had included on our "necessary" list and ferried our friends across the knee-deep Kelly River. (My husband and I had purchased chest-high waders at an army-navy store for six dollars, and tennis shoes from a barrel of oversized shoes for a dollar a pair, his bright yellow and mine bright red.)

No *"dear, dear, dear"* answered our frequent calls on our all-afternoon trek through the forest on the opposite shore. *Spruce grouse* wandered in and out of the low undergrowth. A baby *gyrfalcon* poked its head out of a nest high in a tree. As the day lengthened and we had hiked many miles, our return to camp was anything but cheerful. Gordon went off fishing to catch grayling for our evening meal.

I woke in the middle of the night, which at this latitude was still light from the midnight sun, which rolled along the edge of the horizon. Quietly, I crawled from our tent, tied on tennis shoes, and slowly strolled down the line of the dwarf willows. The warm night was magical, and it seemed that I could almost touch the stars.

We had one more day for our search, but on Sunday the day began with less confidence and a decision to separate. And that plan paid off, as my husband, while resting on a log at mid-morning, heard the *tit*'s call. He blew his whistle three times at the same moment that Gordon also heard the birds; so in minutes we gathered together as three *Siberian tits*, calling *"dear, dear, dear,"* flew into our woodland enclosure, foraging at treetop level.

To our surprise, the three little pink-breasted *tits* swooped down to feed in a low vine tangle near where we stood braced against tall tree trunks, in awe of our sighting. Then they were gone. As suddenly as they had arrived, they disappeared into the impenetrable pine forest, still twittering their *"dear, dear, dear."* Hoping to find the little bird family again, our search continued. But it was not to be.

Our pilot returned for us Monday morning. There were tents to strike, there was trash to bury, there was clothing to be repacked, and there were ashes to be watered down and covered with sand. But we were happy campers.

During the next few years, other birders followed in our footsteps. The Kelly Bar became well known as a dependable *Siberian tit* site.

What fun it had been to explore this beautiful river junction, to wander through a pristine wilderness, to encounter the dwellers of this deep forest home, and at the same time feel at home ourselves! Memories of the song *"dear, dear, dear"* and the sight of the tiny songsters will never be forgotten.

THE SINALOA WREN
(I KNOW YOU'RE THERE, BUT WHERE ARE YOU?)
March 2009

For many years my husband's and my favorite sport was to hop on a plane to find and identify a bird that had wandered into North American territory from its normal home in the world. Now, alone, my urge to set out on a birding adventure had waned. Even the *red-footed falcon* on Martha's Vineyard, a sure thing, had not tempted me.

But in the fall of 2008, in an area of tangled thickets near a small stream on nature reserve property near Patagonia, Arizona, a small, dark brown *Sinaloa wren,* a Mexican species, was happily living. I suppose happily, as the little bird sang its song once every morning at dawn, and continued to be seen by a fortunate few since its discovery by local birder Matt Brown until the winter of 2009, when I was living in nearby Green Valley.

My curiosity got the best of me. The probability of adding a rare bird to my North American bird list loomed before me, and the bird's choice of tangled thickets was only an hour's drive away. Although it would be necessary to cross to the other side of a mountain in early morning, one Saturday in March, I started out before dawn, delayed a breakfast of coffee and muffins until my arrival, parked my van behind a row of early bird vehicles, and joined a dozen other birders who were dressed in heavy jackets against the cold.

The group of birders already patrolling the edge of a narrow roadside creek offered what facts were already known—facts that I would build on in order to increase my chances of actually seeing a *Sinaloa wren.* Three logs crossed the little stream at intervals. Most of the sightings had been of the wren hopping up on one of the logs, where it remained in sight only for a second or two. The bird had sung once that morning, so we knew it was still there. The sun brought warmth and we peeled off our winter wear down to short-sleeved shirts. That day the wren did not show up, nor the next.

The lucky birders over the months had been few and far between, as large numbers had flown in from every corner of the nation. One dedicated birder from Iowa had flown in for four weekends, continuously monitored the area where the bird had most often popped up, and finally, just before his last Sunday's flight deadline, got a good look as it perched momentarily on a log that crossed the creek nearest the road.

The following Saturday I drove back to Patagonia, again before dawn, as otherwise the rising sun would blind me on my journey east. That morning three people sighted the wren as it exposed itself on the most distant log, but only for a few seconds; those of us not in the line of view waited unsuccessfully throughout the rest of the day. I returned Sunday morning to the same sad story.

Instead of being discouraged, now I was determined to devote the rest of the spring, if necessary, to finding that bird. So the next Saturday I departed with a packed overnight bag. If I did not find the bird that day, I would stay overnight at the

Stagecoach Inn in Patagonia. I was tired of making that early morning drive.

The wren had called before my arrival. After spending some time walking along the edge of the road and checking my favorite places for examining the most likely thickets, I unfolded my canvas armchair and confined my search to the three logs in view of my binoculars. There were numerous *Bewick's wrens* skulking about tree roots and confusing the issue. At midmorning, a small brown bird worked around in the bushes across the stream, but we could not get a view of a head with a creamy eyebrow or a dark tail. Then the little bird disappeared into the tall yellow grass in the background. An hour later, the wren hopped onto the nearest log, just as Matt Brown had predicted it would! The *Sinaloa wren*!!

We all tried to follow its activity as the wren disappeared into the streamside tangle, but soon all was silent again. A birding acquaintance from California and I headed for the Patagonia deli for bowls of hot soup. I was tired of a diet of muffins.

As I headed home in early afternoon and neared the intersection of Ruby Road and Interstate Highway 19, in the corner of the Pilot gas station I saw a Wendy's sign. My reward would be a big chocolate Frosty! As I drove north I dug into the delicious cold dessert until the plastic cup was empty.

No champagne for me!

A GUILT TRIP

The *northern lapwing*, an accidental visitor from Europe, is an easily recognizable bird. It has an iridescent dark back, white below, well-demarcated black breast, and prominent wispy crest. A black Rorschach splotch is spattered against a buffy cheek. To me, it is the most handsome *plover.*

So when a *northern lapwing* had landed in a field near St. John's, Newfoundland, my husband, even though he was recuperating in the hospital from surgery, pleaded with me to "go" for the bird. In late afternoon I caught a local airport bus to the Toronto airport. Was I surprised to encounter four birding friends on the same mission? Certainly not. We combined resources, checked into a St. John's motel at two o'clock in the morning, and were out again at six. Coffee and doughnuts from a small bakery, open at this early hour, would do for breakfast on our way to meet our old friend and guide, Bruce McTavish.

The *lapwing* was not in the field where it had been seen daily for a week or more. In spite of our binocular scans and a morning's drive along the few grassy fields in this evergreen-studded coast, no black-and-white *plover* appeared. At noon, with a three o'clock return air ticket in my purse, I decided to go home. My friends begged me to stay another day to help them search for a *greenshank* somewhere in the harbor, but I already felt guilty. They reluctantly returned me to the little airport.

I was in the airport lounge, opening my overnight bag into which I had thrown a small knitting project, needles and yarn in my hand, when Tom Heatley rushed in, shouting for all to hear, "Harriet, come quick! The *lapwing* is HERE!" In bright view in a Questar telescope, I took a long look at the subject of my search in the grass along the edge of the runway. It really was my bird! If I had not insisted on going home, we probably would have missed it.

A year or two later, a flock of sixteen *lapwings* landed in the same field. A radio newscaster somehow heard of the little old lady who had come all the way from the United States to see the *lapwing* that had landed there before. He phoned from St. John's and asked if I would take part in their morning talk show. I said I would. A week later the phone rang, and I answered questions and tried to explain the excitement at finding a new bird.

My friends Max and Helen Parker from Arkansas had flown in to view the birds. As they stood at the edge of the field, now full of *lapwings*, a woman approached and explained, "I heard the lady on the radio talk about these birds, and I decided I should come out to see them."

The Saturday morning I'd been cruising along the Newfoundland coast, my daughter's phone rang. A frantic voice from a friend who knew that her father was in the hospital said, "I can't find your mother!" She was startled to hear my daughter's calm voice reply, "Oh, yeah, my mom's in Newfoundland." That story resurfaced in our community for years. And dispersed by my four companions, the original story also traveled throughout the birding world. I've even had it told to me!

THE BIRD TRAP: LONDON
August 1970

I was tired of hanging around London waiting for friends who were coming to join me for a hostel trip to Switzerland. A walk by the Hyde Park soapbox orators failed to turn up any inspirational messages by the impassioned speakers. A slow saunter through the Burlington Arcade, gazing at the window displays of priceless items out of the reach of my pocketbook, entertained me for a while. Thus two days had gone by, with return visits to Westminster Abbey and the National Gallery.

Then I remembered that all cosmopolitan cities contain dozens of small parks that appear as green areas on city maps, and where there are trees, there would be birds. I was right. On the northwest corner of the London outskirts, I found not only a green area, but the added attraction of the city water reservoir, which certainly would attract waterbirds. And now I had a goal in mind: to find a *great crested grebe,* a species I had seen only once before, on a pond in Norway. It was possible there could be one floating on the broad expanse of the open water tank.

A quick check of the map on the wall of the Underground

station sent me to the black-line route and a fast ride to the end of the line. I emerged into daylight, spotted a small grocery store on the opposite side of the road, and remembered that I'd left my lodging without packing anything to eat. I crossed the road, and in the little shop I found the perfect lunch — a bag of mixed fruit and nuts, which I purchased and stashed in my daypack. I also asked where I could catch a bus, pointing to the city map and the spot I had circled in black ink.

The bus ride was about an hour long. It cruised along streets of a quiet neighborhood of connected cottages, every window protected with white lace curtains. Rosebushes climbed the black iron fences encircling small green gardens. At last the driver indicated my debarkation corner and promised that I would find him there when he returned on his regular route.

I began to walk up a narrow road that led to an enormous water storage tank, easily recognized in the distance by its shape and size. I encountered no one as I climbed up the slanting walls of the concrete tank and, with delight, discovered the moving forms of the waterbirds I had expected to find there. I sat on the broad edge of the vast walls, basked in the noonday sun, and munched on my trail mix. Then with binoculars I studied the bird species bobbing and diving in front of me.

I had had experience in identifying European waterbirds on trips to Greece and Norway, so I happily checked out each familiar species. There were *teal, wigeon, pochard, tufted ducks,* and *shovelers*; and in the center of the reservoir, at last I found the object of my quest: the *great crested grebe.* No doubt about it. The large size, long neck, and crested head were unmistakable.

The afternoon grew hot. On the ground below I noticed people moving about between buildings, but nobody inter-rupted my personal field trip. I noticed trees on the far side of the road that I had followed into the facility, so I decided to walk over there to look for a *European goldfinch,* a bird species I hadn't seen in many years. Carefully descending the slanting side of the storage tank, I had almost reached the road when a park vehicle appeared, driven by a uniformed guard and carrying two enormous dogs in a cage on the back of the truck.

His eyes registered surprise. He lowered the truck window and asked, "What are you doing here?"

I explained.

He laughed, "Didn't you see the warning sign at the entrance?"

I hadn't.

Again he laughed. "Lady, you have my permission to look for the *goldfinches.* Good luck." And he drove off as the vicious-looking dogs barked and lunged about in their confining cage.

I spent an hour in the woods, found the *goldfinches,* and headed for the bus stop for my return trip to London center. As I approached the the main road, I turned back to look for the warning sign. It was there, all right, though quite unobtrusive and near the ground. On granite stone was carved: TRESPASSERS FORBIDDEN. GROUNDS PATROLLED BY DOGS!

THE LONG, LONG TRAIL
TO LITTLE BARRIER ISLAND
January 1993

Twenty-five kilometers off the east coast of New Zealand lies Little Barrier Island, the only home of the *stitchbird*, where a permit from the Department of Conservation is required to land. But unless you are a research scientist, no amount of pleading will get you the paper document needed to land on its shores. We tried!

Many years earlier we had been more fortunate, when the department officials granted us a day pass to the island of Kapiti. From the seaside village of Paraparaumu, just after dawn, a fisherman in a small vessel carried us the short distance across the bay to the spectacularly steep island, which rises 1,780 feet above sea level. We had to wade ashore, but we were greeted by a friendly resident ranger who directed us to the start of a track to the summit. It was bush-covered and of rough terrain; however, we persevered up the steep incline, often stopping to rest, until we reached the very top, where we looked down into a blue lagoon and out to the endless sea. What a great lunch stop on top of the world!

Along the way we had seen the rare *saddleback* and a *long-tailed cuckoo* and encountered our first *tuis* and a tiny *whitehead* in the forest canopy.

Our second lucky strike during our birding in New Zealand was finding a boat that regularly crossed the bay to Tiritiri, an island covered with broom, fern, and gorse. On the track from the beach up to the ranger station we found *brown teal* swimming on a little pond and *brown quail* sunning themselves beside the path, apparently not afraid of people. The resident (captive) *takahe* strutted across the lawn around the building. We reached a forest of small trees, where all afternoon we happily lingered in the midst of *bellbirds, yellow-* and *red-crested parrots*, a very shining *green cuckoo, saddlebacks* scuttling into grassy verges, a rifleman calling a high-pitched *"zit, zit, zit"* (so faint one was lucky to hear him at all), and our old friend the *whitehead*. *White-fronted terns* fluttered along the coastline.

Only the rarest of birds, the *stitchbird*, was beyond our reach.

Then one day near the end of our stay at the Bay of Islands, we drove to the nearby town of Kerikeri to shop for groceries. Our efforts to get in touch with a local expert birder had failed, and now we decided to make one last try by phone. New Zealand's wonderful telephone system, especially helpful for visitors, allowed us to purchase a phone card that enabled us to call anywhere in the country. The phones were located on corners around the towns, and we used them a lot.

I began my search for a corner phone but did not see one in the vicinity. I am the kind of person who is not embarrassed to ask for help, so I entered an office building and explained why I wished to find the nearest phone, and, like all New Zealanders we met, these were more than helpful.

They asked if I had heard about Captain Jerry Clark, a now famous resident, who had sailed in his small boat, the

Totorore, to the tip of South Africa, set out to return alone, and had been given up for lost, when his little sailboat drifted into the Auckland harbor with a remaining sail the size of a tattered handkerchief. He wrote a book about the adventure, and the copies were already sold out.

Captain Clark was presently out to sea leading an ornithological cruise, but our informers thought that maybe his wife, who lived only a few blocks away next to the stone bridge, could help out.

Mrs. Clark not only sent us on our way to an extraordinary adventure, but she invited us in for tea and freshly baked cookies. As we talked about our experiences on North Island, she remembered that she had a good friend who, with her son, had built a sailboat and offered day trips in the offshore waters. She phoned June. They had just finished the last trip of the season and were about to put up the sailboat, but she agreed that if we could get to Whangaroa the next morning, they would take us out to sea. We did.

So began one of the most remarkable days of pelagic birding we have ever known. Very soon June realized that we were not interested in her prepared lectures about the island's early history. She relaxed. Then she and her nineteen-year-old son gave themselves over to our excitement, turned their vessel out into deep water, and enthusiastically scanned the teeming flocks of *white-faced storm petrels, Buller's* and *fluttering shearwaters,* a *gannet, Caspian terns, black-headed gulls,* and *white-fronted terns.*

June brought out delicious scones at midmorning, and later a lunch of veggie quiche. Instead of their spending the day entertaining us, we entertained them, and they loved it, caught up in our delight with everything around us — the beautiful day itself, the little boat, the flocks of seabirds constantly circling in the air and along the tips of the waves, good food, and, as we must eventually return to land, the end of a perfect day.

We told them of our disappointment at not being able to visit Little Barrier Island, so near and yet so far. But wait—June's friend, captain of the tourist ship the *Te Aroha*, offered weekend cruises around the islands, and once a month he was permitted to land his passengers on Little Barrier Island. When we reached shore, June phoned the captain, who, unbelievably, was going to stop at Little Barrier Island that very weekend. Would he have room for us? He did! Our only problem was our scheduled flight to Fiji the evening of our return. The captain solved the problem, promising to have a taxi waiting for us at the dock.

The *Te Aroha* might have been a replica of Columbus's *Pinta* or *Santa Maria*, with its thick wooden hull and interior bunks, tables, and benches. All day Friday we steamed among the off-shore islands. At last, on Saturday morning, our ship anchored off Little Barrier Island, where we were rowed ashore in a dory, and we leaped to the sandy shore with more excitement than I could ever remember.

The day was lovely, sunny and warm. And in addition to our phenomenal luck at being there, our guide was Geoff Moon, author of *The Reed Field Guide to New Zealand Birds*, a volume of exquisite bird photographs. After a half hour of slowly walking an ever-ascending forest trail, Geoff called out, and I found the *stitchbird* in a flock of small birds. To me it resembled a small *honeyeater.* How could such a tiny creature create such a feeling of awe in its very presence on this small island, now protected from predators by governmental decree? I watched until the little bird disappeared as the flock moved on through the trees.

This had been a superb birding day, but reluctantly we returned to the *Te Aroha* to sail amid flocks of *Cook's petrels*, so close I could see their grizzly gray foreheads, back to Auckland and the waiting taxi.

I never did find the corner telephone!

BEN AND I
May 1988

Ben King is acknowledged as the supreme authority on the birds of southeast Asia as, since his service in World War II, he has spent his entire birding life as a guide in that region. Ben's reputation as a tough, hard-core, demanding ogre is legend — leading birders in long days tramping or climbing (regardless of the weather, and late for dinner), or midnight hours spent straining necks to the treetops in response to owl calls.

Let me tell you about the Ben I know after being his shadow in Thailand, Burma, India, the Andamans, Hong Kong, the Philippines, and even Attu Island, when, though I was not a part of his tour, he escorted me into Henderson Valley to see the *bean goose* I'd missed the day before.

Nitalvas, monarchs, hornbills, minias, fulvettas, plus the ever-present *verditor flycatcher*: These birds do not turn up in our back-yards.

In May 1988, I joined Ben's tour of West China and Tibet. Our ultimate target was the *Temminck's tragopan,* a bird that is found only in the mountains of Tibet, Burma, and Yunnan Province in China. The government of China does not welcome visitors who do not follow their tourist-oriented itineraries, but Ben had arranged for the China Forest Service to care for us, a small group of three. From Chengdu, the capital of Sichuan Province, two vehicles were provided—one for our birding group and one for a small staff, which in addition to the drivers included two cooks and a young female interpreter whose command of English was based on a six-week language course.

There was a mountain tunnel to crawl through, thin mattresses filled with straw ticking, narrow swinging bridges that connected small villages to the woodlands on the other side of rivers, and noon stir-fry meals at open-fronted roadside stands. We even kicked up chunks of ice with our boots on early morning walks along mountain streams.

We arrived at the Wolong National Nature Reserve, a panda preserve where there actually were a few baby pandas that had been rescued after the deaths of their mothers. Even though our limbs ached from the long afternoon climb, no one stayed behind at the hostel when Ben started to cross the swinging bridge over the moving river below and loped toward a forested summit. Our eyes took in a narrow trail, probably used by the natives on their way to work in the fields far below. Ben whispered, "*Golden pheasant,* watch the end of the trail!" Maybe ten or fifteen minutes passed. We were silent with anticipation. Then the most beautiful bird I had ever seen slowly crossed the trail, his golden feathers highlighted by the evening sun. Our adventure had begun!

When we tired of hiking, there were intervals of hunching together under cover of bushes waiting for the birds to come to us. This is called "people watching." After a picnic on a hot day, I loved the naps under a forest tree, my head resting on a pillow of soft moss. Or afternoon teatime, served oudoors by our cook on a folding table with cloth and silverware. At Lushan National Park in Jiangxi, where hot water was available only from seven to seven-thirty in the evening, Ben made sure that our cook served dinner early so we could bathe in the steaming hot water in deep iron tubs. Ben's soft voice often offered me the choice of resting on a fallen log or big rock while the others forged ahead, but there was his shadow again, following ever upward, sometimes aware of fresh panda spore on the path. Did you know that scientists can tell the age of a panda by the length of the straw-like bamboo they excrete?

When I am asked—and I often am—which is my favorite bird, I readily answer, *"Temminck's tragopan."* I am not certain whether it is because of the beauty of this mountain *pheasant* or its remoteness and the effort needed to find one. In spite of close contenders—the *shoebill, ibisbill, wallcreeper,* and *brown kiwi*—the *tragopan* remains my favorite bird of all time.

The assault began with a three o'clock in the morning wake-up call, breakfast carried in a brown bag, and a very steep climb for about two hours, with mini-flashlights lighting the trail ahead. Not a sound was heard except for the occasional shifting of a disturbed rock or a stumbled footstep. Eventually the land leveled off and the ascent became easier. Still Ben's stride never slackened. He knew the importance of arriving at the top while the world was still asleep.

At the end of the climb, in the darkness the outlines of my companions were hardly visible. Then Ben in his alertness heard something: A movement? An early morning bird call? He played a short, soft measure from a small tape recorder. Then, at the first glow of approaching dawn, unaware of our presence, the most unimaginably breathtaking bird walked into view, circled a low bush, continued on its circling journey, then disappeared. I had studied images of this most striking of creatures, the extremely bright orange body smothered with white spots, the gorgeous blue facial skin that expanded into hanging lappets marked with bright red patches, black feathers encircling the face. But in those few moments, the vision was a blur of almost phosphorescent color, too much to absorb. Wait!! The show was not over! As we stood transfixed, the *tragopan* once again crossed an open space at our feet and then was gone.

There isn't much more to say, except to explain that over the years the ogre didn't seem to mind his shadow—uphill, downhill, fording streams on mossy logs, trudging along jungle trails, or crossing the flat-topped world of grassland under cloudless skies.

I owe some of the most spectacular moments of my birding life to Ben, and I've lived to tell the tale.

CHASING PENGUINS
1981; 1984; 1993; 1995; 1997

My first sighting of a penguin was through a glass window at the Detroit Zoo Penguinarium in summertime, though those sleek, graceful, gliding creatures normally spend their lives in the icy waters of the southern hemisphere. I stood there, fascinated, and wondered if I could identify penguins in the wild. This thought was ridiculous, as penguin species are very different from one another when you get to know them.

The year 1981 was a very good one for penguins—and for me. To celebrate our fortieth wedding anniversary, my husband and I had signed up for a thirty-five-day circumnavigation of Antarctica aboard the ship the *World Discoverer*. The tour began with both bad and good luck, as you will see. The bad luck actually threatened to cancel the whole tour when, in Puntas Arenas, Chile, our departure point, a boilerplate broke. The good luck was that, while waiting three days for an engineer to fly from Germany bringing a replacement, the tour operators arranged to send us by bus on daylong sightseeing trips.

Thus, *Magellanic* penguins became our first contact with these unique birds. *Magellanic* penguins breed on the coast of Argentina and the Falkland Islands, but a few weeks before our arrival, a farmer had discovered a colony in one of his fields only a few miles from the Chilean harbor. Bad luck that the buses sank into mud up to their hubcaps. Good luck that boxed chicken dinners had been sent along. Bad luck that it took the rest of the day to pull the heavy vehicles out of the muddy field. Good luck for us that the curious *Magellanics* popped out of their burrows and stared at us from their doorways. They had never seen such a sight!

Our ship finally took to sea, cruised down the Beagle Channel, rounded Cape Horn in calm waters, and steamed away toward the Antarctica Peninsula.

A series of landings along the snow-covered shore began. Wearing a bright orange windbreaker, as if I could get lost among the penguin flocks against a snowy background, I stood at the edge of colonies of *adelie, chinstrap,* and *gentoo* penguins called *brushtails* because their stiff tail feathers stick out behind them when they walk. These penguins are circumpolar, as we encountered them everywhere: *adelies,* diving into white-capped waves; the fuzzy young of *gentoos* chasing parents, begging for food; and *chinstraps,* the second most abundant penguin species, with their narrow band of black feathers below snowy white chin and cheeks.

Our ship then set out for the shelf of the Antarctic continent, where so many countries claim ownership that, at present, an international agency supervises overall activities. After stopping at Russian, Polish, and Argentinian stations, and a visit to the United States' Palmer Station, we reached McMurdo Sound, headquarters for all Antarctic explorations.

Their summer of scientific experiments had just ended, and

except for the over-wintering staff, all other personnel had departed on the last navy icebreaker to leave for the winter. We walked to nearby Scott Base, the green-painted headquarters of the ill-fated Scott expedition to the South Pole. We moved among the temperature-controlled buildings and talked to the scientists about their projects, one of which was a study of fish that were able to exist in the icy saltwater of the sound. And all around us were flocks of penguins, thousands of little dark figures against the snow and icy fields.

Maybe my best luck of the entire trip came the night we left McMurdo Sound and proceeded to round Cape Adare. No *emperor* penguins had been sighted on previous Lindblad Antarctic cruises because the *emperor* breeds in early winter, nesting on the inland ice. But I had heard that the tip of Cape Royds was our only, slim chance of finding one on the ice floes floating along at the edge of the shore.

As I sat at a table prepared for a six-course dinner, where through the porthole I could discern the outline of the jagged continent, I folded my napkin, placed it on the table, and queried my husband, "Why are we sitting here?" He followed me up onto the top deck, where we leaned against the ship's rail and listened to the cracking sounds below as the ice field broke into giant slabs. But not more than fifteen minutes after our arrival on deck, an announcement rang out over the loudspeaker: "*Emperor* penguins on starboard side!"

And there they were! Two huge erect *emperor* penguins, riding along on a floating ice floe. Barely had we had time to admire them, when, as the ship neared, they silently slid backward and sank out of sight. The diners below probably didn't realize what they had missed; but when we returned to our table, grinning with satisfaction, they were happy for us.

After rounding the tip of the continent, we continued to

sail through brash ice and twenty-stories-high tubular icebergs. *Wilson's storm-petrels* danced above the waves, like butterflies, their toes scarcely touching the water. Leopard seals slept on moving ice islands. Daily, we were surrounded by *black-browed albatross* and *giant, Antarctic, pintado,* and *snow petrels.* Finally, we arrived at Macquarie Island, an Australian protectorate.

Our first sight on entering the harbor, on a rocky promontory, was a colony of *rockhopper* penguins, their yellow bristly hair tufts sticking straight up, crowded onto rocky shelves, actually hopping on their bright yellow feet from one ledge to another.

Happy as we were to see the *rockhoppers,* we had come to find the *royal* penguins, which had chosen Hurd Point, on the tip of the island, as their breeding ground. Five hundred thousand pairs, with crest-like yellow head feathers, were packed so tightly together that, during the breeding season, vegetation disappeared and chicks were raised in mud.

Only a few of our ship's landing party dared to crawl over and around the huge, jutting coastal rocks, often with deep watery caverns roaring below in the abysses we had to jump over. After tiptoeing along the sand in front of enormous elephant seals that lifted their strange-looking heads, seeming ready to lunge, then snuffled and sank back into lethargy, we at last reached the end of the boulder-strewn shore. I could hardly believe the size of the *royal* colony that stretched in front of me. The young were in all stages of molt, quite ugly children at this stage. This was our only chance to see this species of penguin, and the dangerous journey along the inhospitable beach and back again had been a brilliant success.

The next bad luck brought us an unexpected good-luck adventure when the government of Australia sent a message that only seventy passengers would be allowed to land on Campbell Island.

With one hundred and ten passengers on board, there was no way to handle such a situation except by drawing lots, so a request was sent to the New Zealand government for permission to land on their possession, Enderby Island. It was granted.

Crewmen with shuffleboard paddles protected us from the ornery sea lions on the beach. Here was our first sight of greenery since leaving South America. Green grass, bushes, and a small stand of stunted trees—in addition to a warm gentle breeze—welcomed us. Another welcome sight were the *tomtit, red-crowned parakeet*, and *red-bill gulls*. Land birds, ho!

We had had no preparation for this landing, so our first goal was to find a nest of one of the largest seabirds in the world, a *royal albatross*. When we returned from the nest, which we found with the huge bird sitting on it, we heard a racket of squawking such as I had never heard before. It was coming from a ditch, out of which waddled a line of six *yellow-eyed* penguins loudly singing off-key! Only a person who had heard such a raucous melody would believe it. The Maori name for the bird means "noise shouter."

While we were viewing the *yellow-eye* parade, on a piece of grassland adjacent to our landing area posed a single *erect-crested* penguin, the least studied, rarest, and most mysterious of penguin species. What a surprise! With its chocolate brown eyes, it is the only penguin that can raise and lower the upward sweeping crests of long, brush-like feathers. It climbs steep rock faces to breed on ledges and platforms.

Our cruise ended in Christchurch, New Zealand, after thirty-six days at sea—too long for some travelers, because, as far as I know, this tour has never been repeated. Of the hundred and ten passengers, at the beginning we were the only birders; but during the long, endless days at sea, a group of converted birders had daily joined us on deck or rushed into the lounge to consult our collection of field guides. We had had company.

During our ten-day stay in New Zealand, we hit real bad luck when we spent a day at Milford Sound, home of the *fjord-land crested* penguin. Twice we took the big boat cruise around the lake and checked every nook and cranny of the coastal ledges, to no avail. Shortly before our arrival, according to the captain, the penguins had been plentiful, sitting out in open cavities around the lake, but he had not seen any for several weeks. Ever optimistic, we had hoped for a late departure by just one bird. But we had to give up!

We crossed the straits to Australia. And one evening, from the grandstand near the beach at Melbourne, we witnessed the nightly return of the *little blue* penguins to their nests, scurrying from the safety of the sea, across the beach, under the bleachers, and up to their burrows. They are also called *fairy* penguins, and they mate for life and dig long, deep burrows where rock crevices are not available.

So, *bang, bang,* we had already seen ten species of penguins, more than half of the world's total supply of seventeen.

It was a few years before I encountered another penguin species, while on a boat trip off the coastal town of Paracas, Peru, in 1984. Our small vessel zigzagged in and out of inlets and naturally hewn stone arches among offshore islands, revealing gaudy *guanay* and *red-legged cormorants* perched on rocky headlands. Then, as we slipped through a wide crack where the sea and wind had eroded the shore, we found gray, colorless *Humboldt* penguins. Only one black neckband separates it from the *Magellanic,* which has two. The *Humboldt* is the friendliest of penguins; when we neared, they did not dive away. They are named for the cold Humboldt Current that flows along the west coast of South America and are the penguins least understood by scientists.

Almost ten years elapsed before my trip to the Galapagos Islands in 1993. Families of *Galapagos* penguins, the most northerly penguin, dwelling in warm water, clustered along the coastal rocks. They hold their flippers out to help heat escape from their bodies and prevent their feet from getting sunburned. I am not kidding. An upside-down-horseshoe-shaped black band decorates its chest.

Two years later, in 1995, we joined a group of British birders aboard a Russian oceanographic vessel to visit the Falkland Islands and South Georgia. *King* penguins had dotted the coast along the way, but now flocks covered the hillsides and swam in the ocean by the thousands. Beautifully dressed, they walked along as if they were businessmen going to their offices, often so friendly that they strolled up and pecked at one's pant leg. On the beach, we were surrounded by groups of *kings* in pairs or small groups. Around the ship, they swam with their heads held high out of the water.

Many birders have been lucky to see *macaroni* penguins near the Antarctica Peninsula, but not I. Though *macaroni* penguins are the most numerous of the species, with five and a half million pairs estimated in South Georgia and the Falklands, even along the coast they keep to the inland bays and breed on rock walls hidden from the ocean. So our rubber raft had to drift into a cove at Cooper Bay to observe the *macaronis* sunning themselves on rocks. *Macaronis* differ from *royals*: the *macaronis* have black faces.

We crossed the South Atlantic, braving a four-day storm at sea. Everything that was not tied down went crashing to the deck. But at the end of our voyage, at the tip of South Africa, on the Cape of Good Hope, it was not difficult to locate the *jackass* penguins our first morning on land. They played hide-and-seek along the boulder-strewn strand, but there really was no place to conceal themselves from us. For all intents and purposes, this would be our last penguin species.

In my wildest dreams I never imagined that I would see a *Snares Island* penguin, until I read about the Heritage Expedition's ship leaving New Zealand for a birding cruise to Campbell, Macquarie, Enderby, Chatham, and Snares Islands. Not daunted by the long flight back Down Under, our hopes of finding this out-of-the-way bird were high. Plus, this would give us another opportunity to visit Milford Sound.

My husband and I flew into Christchurch three days before our sailing departure and drove directly to Milford Sound. This time it was November, a much better chance to see a *fjordland crested* penguin; so we eagerly boarded the cruise boat, our third sweep of the sound, and circled the water, edging close to its indented shore. But again we could not find a penguin lingering on its front doorstep.

We did not give up. Near the dock we noticed a young man working on a little sailboat. We asked him if he would take us sailing along the shore. He did, and at last we drifted into several sheltered coves where *fjordland crested* penguins nested, and in each one a penguin posed, so close that even I could photograph them with my small Konica camera. It isn't often one gets a second chance to search for a special and remote bird. I won't ever forget my cruises around Milford Sound.

Snares Island was to be our first stop on the Heritage Expedition island cruise. I almost would have had to end this story on a sad note because, in the high winds and waves, the captain hesitated to send the inflated rubber rafts ashore. But in late afternoon he gave the order and we paddled the Zodiacs into a hidden cove, where hundreds of these unique penguins live together near the beach.

This moment and the memory of this adventure are unbelievably emotional for me. Even with Campbell, Chatham, and return visits to Macquarie and Enderby ahead, this remote little island, chosen by a family of penguins with a twist of hair tufts from bill to ear to be their home, would always exist in my memory as a magical scene at the edge of the world. I sailed away contented.

In order: *Magellanic, adele, chinstrap, gentoo, emperor, rockhopper, royal, yellow-eyed, erect-crested, little blue, Humboldt, Galapagos, macaroni, king, jackass, fjordland crested,* and *Snare's Island.*

What had started as a simple Antarctic cruise had led us to years of adventures: successes and disappointments, lasting friendships, awareness of protecting our worldwide natural heritage, and a lifetime love of penguins—all seventeen species. But I have to admit, the little *Snares Island* penguin is my favorite.

What a record!

LINES OF COMMUNICATION
May–July 1984

Before the days when computers were household items, the Houston, Texas, Audubon chapter offered for a small fee a subscription to a rare-bird alert called NARBA (North American Rare Bird Alert), based on a series of telephone messages passed from one birder to another. It was not unusual for my husband's law-office secretary to answer the phone to an urgent "Tell Mr. Davidson there is a *yellow grosbeak* at Laguna Atascosa." (Laguna Atascosa is a park in Texas.) In fact, she did not make a startled dash for the inner office, but took these calls with composure. And my job was to find an affordable method of transportation that did not require seven days' notice.

In May 1984, my husband and I had just finished a ten-day campout on the Dry Tortugas, islands ninety miles off the coast of south Florida, when word reached us from a birder visiting High Island, Texas, on a day trip that a *Yucatan vireo* had been discovered there.

This little bird, dark gray with a dark line through its black eye and a white stripe above it, inhabits dry forests, mangrove forests, and shrubland in Mexico! And this was its first venture into the United States, a record highly valued by birders.

Impossible to go for it. This would be very much out of the way on our drive back to Michigan, where we had only a few days to pack for a campout on Attu Island, in the Aleutian Islands in Alaska. So we flew off Bush Key in the little seaplane and began the drive north—as far as Lake City, Florida, that is. There two highways diverged: Interstate 75 north, nonstop to Detroit, and Interstate 10 west, across Alabama, Mississippi, and Louisiana to Texas. Neither of us spoke a word as my husband turned west; it would be an all-night drive, but there were two of us.

We arrived at High Island in late afternoon the following day, with pretty explicit directions as to the *vireo*'s location—clumps of small bushes where the little bird had been seen on and off all day. An hour went by, and daylight was fading when our target bird perched in the open long enough for my husband to get a photo. As we turned to leave, a young lady approached and handed him a piece of paper with her name and address and a request for a copy of the bird's picture. We said good-bye and hurried on our way.

In July that summer, we received a postcard from our young friend, who was between semesters at college, working as an assistant naturalist with the U.S. National Park Service in the Chiricahua Mountains in the Coronado National Forest of southeast Arizona, an area known as Sky Island. I still remember the closing of her thank-you for the *vireo* photo: "It is very quiet here. The only bird we have is a *berylline* hummingbird." One of our most-wanted species, endemic to Mexico and an infrequent visitor to the United States!

On a previous abortive attempt to find the *berylline*, we had flown into Tucson, Arizona, made the two-hour drive to Miller Canyon, where we remained all afternoon, quiet and alert, sitting on a hillside patch of grass that bordered a swale, but where now a *magnificent* hummingbird had taken charge and had chased away the smaller hummers. We had missed that bird by only hours.

So this *berylline* hummingbird was a piece of cake on an early morning walk along a curve in the road in the Chiricahuas. As the emerald-green bird with chestnut wings and tail, not as flashy as some hummingbird species, moved steadily from one low plant to another at the edge of the highway, I was amazed that anybody had discovered this tiny bird at all.

Birders' lines of communication have changed drastically with online bird alerts, not only nationwide but statewide and locally, too. We've gone from scribbling down directions that often led us into strange, unchartered byways, to using Google Earth, which pinpoints the spot we are headed for. I call it evolution.

PART II
ALASKA

HOME AT HALIBUT COVE
July 1973

H i there, Clem. I've brought some friends to meet you," Gene Foss shouted from the deck of the marine ferry the *Tustumenma* as it sidled up to the dock at Homer, Alaska. It was noon, and after three rainy days on Kodiak Island, the sun shone with welcome brightness and warmth.

We looked down to see a tall, red-haired stranger wearing a striped jumpsuit, lounging against the rail and watching the deckhands secure the ferry. Clem was not entirely a stranger, as we had written to him in response to his brief advertisement in Alaska's travel booklet *Off the Beaten Track*, and in his answer he had informed us that he ran a daily ferry to Kachemak Bay. According to our research, this was an uninhabited, undeveloped national park, just what we were looking for.

His little launch was about to depart on the afternoon tour. "We're not ready," we protested, having just arrived from our campground at Kenai.

"Come along for the ride," he invited, starting the motor. "We'll find a campsite and I'll take you back this evening.

Besides," he added, "I'll take you near some rock islands where you can get some good pictures." His engaging grin and hints of adventure convinced us. We took the bait and, leaving our station wagon in the parking lot, my husband and I and two teenage boys—our son Matt and his friend Jeff—clambered onto the ferry.

Thus began our friendship with Clem Tillion. Clem knew the names of all the seabirds around us. When he called out *"Marbled murrelets!"* we shifted our binoculars in time to see the dark backs of the *alcids* skittering away on the surface of the bay. He slowed down near gull rocks to point out *red-faced cormorants*—large, gawky, long-necked, rather fierce hooked-billed birds—alert as they shifted about on scraggly nests. The clownish round outlines and painted red-and-yellow bills of their neighbors, the *horned puffins,* accentuated the *cormorants'* angular coal-black shapes. "Watch for surfbirds on the rocks by the dock!" Without this advance warning, we could have missed the gray-and-white splotches against gray-and-white rocks.

True to his promise, Clem, in the evening twilight, returned us to a deserted shore that the four of us had chosen for our camp. And that is how we found our home at Halibut Cove.

Halibut Cove, a quarter mile of shoreline bounded on both sides by rocky promontories, was home from the first moment we sighted it. The escarpment provided no level spot for a campsite, though the boys managed to erect their backpack tents on a bushy slope. My husband was able to rig a transparent plastic tarpaulin over our two sleeping bags on the bluff. The boys, both Eagle Scouts, built a fire bowl on the gravel beach above the high-tide line; dry firewood abounded in the spruce forest; and giant rocks and driftwood logs served as tables and chairs. We were settled in before the sinking sun set fire to the clouds along the horizon.

In the morning a sei whale came to play in our oceanfront, and two leopard seals with beady eyes surfaced to keep track of our activities. On a nearby log, a golden-brown squirrel, bushy tail curled over his back and a nut between his paws, joined us for breakfast. The dark western race of the oversized *song sparrow* hopped in and out of the bushes that outlined our dining room. Housekeeping chores quickly finished, we pulled on waders and cast into the surf for whatever fish might be most gullible.

Ocean tides rise and fall twice each day. Occasionally, there are extremely low tides, and these are best for clam digging. The morning after our moving in we had the lowest tide of all: minus five. Arriving by boat, Clem brought us a bucket and shovel. The sand gurgled and popped, tiny jets of water squirted everywhere, and starfish lay helplessly draped on the rocks. We dashed back and forth, digging at the telltale holes with little success until, by trial and error, we discovered that big deep holes exposed our quarry rather well. Our buckets were full of clams before the rising tide forced us to retreat. The next morning we had a minus-three tide and expertly dug up a new supply. What banquets as the pile of clamshells grew around us as we dined by the campfire!

Never having reckoned with tides before, we continually forgot our dependence upon them. At high tide we could not cross the cove and had to confine our exploring to the shore. At low tide our boundaries extended far out to sea and the bay was spotted with dark pine-covered islands.

Clem loaned the boys a small skiff and motor so that they could explore the coves and fish for salmon. One day we took the skiff to another cove. This meant encountering the rough waters of Kachemak Bay three different times while exposing ourselves to rocky headlands in our little outboard, but Jeff efficiently guided our small craft through the swells, while Matt, the coxswain, took so much spray over the bow that we had to put him ashore temporarily to build a fire and dry himself out.

Jeff was the first to hook a big salmon, which thrashed and ran until Jeff at last eased him close to the boat, where we captured it with a net. With only a six-pound line, I reeled in a two-footer. The four of us fished all afternoon, outmaneuvering the powerful sea creatures, but we returned them unharmed so that they could swim back to their spawning grounds later in the summer. At the crest of high tide, we sailed home by sliding over the sandbars, and relaxed while the clams and salmon simmered on the campfire under the golden canopy of evening.

Another day the boys took us by skiff across the bay to a far shore, where my husband and I hiked over a forested pass to an ancient glacier. Our trail led us through a jungle of moss-dripping spruce, shoulder-high wood fern, and decaying logs. At first we climbed steeply, and then the ground leveled off and we entered a tundra meadow before abruptly descending onto a moonscaped alluvial plain. From the dark woods, we emerged into the glare of blue-white glacial ice. In every direction, boulders lay, as if some playful giant had tossed them at random over a mile-long prehistoric football field. Like dwarfs, we picked our way through the primeval chaos, closer and closer to the glacier until, at last, we peered down into a silver-blue lake fed by the receding ice.

In our isolation, absorbing the silent strength of the primordial elements around us, we mere mortals perched in sunshine on top of one of the giant's toys and ate our picnic lunch.

On our return journey along the forest edge, we met a family of *spruce grouse*. When I lifted my binoculars to scan an overhanging stone cliff, I was astonished to gaze into the unblinking eyes of two perched fledgling *horned owls*! The mother obviously didn't trust me, because from deep in the woods, in low cooing tones, she coaxed her children to clumsily flap away to join her. We continued on, rattling keys and singing songs to warn the bears to keep away.

To our dismay, the tide caught us unprepared. The beach where the boys had left us was now exposed twenty feet below, far out in the bay. Scout know-how solved our problem. On a ladder of lashed tree roots, scrunching under and clinging to alder branches, we lowered ourselves onto a ledge where the boys could later rescue us when they returned in the skiff.

Was there ever an end to a day at Halibut Cove? Mornings were opening eyes to the gulls and terns patrolling the shore and the ever-changing tides. Days were without time, nights without darkness. Our eyes encountered a hundred shades of blue and a thousand shades of green. A scolding ground squirrel. Breakfast around a campfire. Freedom to wander.

But we had to say farewell, and one morning we shouldered our backpacks, hiked over the trail to Clem's ferry, and caught a ride back to the real world. Clem had kept his promise. He had put us ashore on one of our country's most beautiful, out-of-the-way national parks, and for a brief sojourn we had made it our home.

HOME ON THE DESHKA RIVER
August 1973

In Alaska the bush pilot is a necessary accessory to cross-country transportation, linking native villages to centers of population, government, and industry and ferrying thousands of adventurers into remote regions to fish or hunt. Dave, our pilot, was a very young man, but ages old in flying experience. We felt the assurance with which he taxied his Cessna-135 float plane over the water of Lake Hood, gently lifted us above the inlet, then leveled off into tundra country, dotted with thousands of tiny ponds, marshes, and occasional spruce forests. It was late afternoon and we (my husband, Matt, Jeff, and I) were on our way to the Deshka River to float downstream in rubber rafts.

It was our good fortune that Mike Hershberger, writer, local fisherman, and guide, had decided he could squeeze our weekend into his busy summer schedule, and we became acquainted over piles of rafts, backpacks, fishing rods, and food rations. After our pilot deposited us on the shore of a small lake, a short hike through the woods, portaging all the gear, brought us to the river, where

Mike and the boys inflated two rubber rafts—bright yellow for Matt and Jeff, black for us adults—then stacked the duffel on tent-pole crossbars. I pulled on my hip boots.

The boys pushed off and we soon followed. Hanging clouds obscured the former sunny skies but did not dampen our expectant spirits. In early August, Alaska's midnight sun had not been seen for several weeks; nevertheless, twilight lingered until after ten o'clock. Mike, at the bow, dipped his paddle now and then in order to keep our craft from swinging into sweepers, the downed trees and roots reaching out to grab the unwary. Occasionally it was necessary for him to swing himself overboard to rope the raft through shallows. The boys bobbed ahead of us, efficient pilots, perched fore and aft on the raft's bright bumpers.

Our evening idyll ended abruptly as Mike sighted a long gravel bar. Darkness was definitely approaching, and it was time to pitch tents and cook dinner. The canvas tent rose marvelously high, with enough headroom for even my six-foot husband, and the hamburgers broiled over a campfire tasted better than any hamburgers I had ever eaten before. No sounds from the forest disturbed our sleep.

The next morning we were awakened by Mike's shout, "Who wants a cup of coffee?" and I was half out of my sleeping bag almost before he had finished the sentence. The second sound I heard forecast the day's weather: rain on the roof. Fresh deep tracks of bear and moose imprinted the surrounding soft sand. Mike had left the beach fire blazing through the night to ward off unwelcome wild visitors. He served up pancakes and brown sugar syrup and then we leisurely broke camp. Ahead lay a whole day to float and fish.

Alaska's rivers flowed along unusually low this year; frequently Mike and my husband both had to paddle to make headway. We regularly jumped out to fish the swirling deep holes under rocks and logs, returning the small trout and grayling after we'd had the fun of outwitting them.

No matter how vigorously Matt and Jeff paddled, they could not outdo Mike's skillful propelling of our raft. From many summers of guiding fishermen on Alaska's trophy waters, Mike had become an expert. Sometime in early afternoon, we halted to make sandwiches of brown bread, cheese, and sausage. About the same time, the light rain changed from intermittent showers into a steady downpour! It beat an insistent tattoo on our rain jackets, jetted off our rain hats, gathered in puddles at our feet. Mike, my husband, and the boys absorbed a good quantity of it as they lifted their arms rhythmically to paddle, and even though I was curled up comfortably behind Mike in the bow, eventually the drops trickled through to my down vest. Sometimes we beached the rafts and fished.

During a slight lull in the weather, Mike started a roaring fire on a sandbar and everybody dried out. Mike's jeans hissed steam when he inched dangerously close to the orange flames; my husband dangled his wool shirt and jacket until they were thoroughly smoke-drenched; the boys ignored their discomfort, but announced that they were hungry. So Mike fried ham slices and hash browns in the glowing coals. It is amazing how one's outlook on life improves when one is warm and well fed! We eradicated all traces of our intrusion on the land and embarked again on the Deshka River.

We drifted and paddled downstream. As the evening shadows lengthened, we began looking for a suitable sandbar, one large enough for our big tent, Mike's big backpack, and lots of driftwood. Once we investigated a sand spit that was covered with very fresh bear tracks the size of a large frying pan. Mike suggested that we go on to the next bar! Which we did, except that in the next hour the river widened and no built-up stretch of gravel appeared. This was odd, since we had grown accustomed to finding a sandbar around every bend in the river. We floated on and on. Darkness fell. A great horned owl hooted from deep in the woods Another owl joined in. The spooky hoots reassured us that we were not traveling alone.

Still no gravel bars. Matt and Jeff dropped back to paddle close to us, but finally we dispatched them to patrol the far shore, until their little raft became a barely discernible blur of gold. We proceded slowly, Mike sweeping his paddle back and forth to avoid sharp rocks and fallen trees that could puncture our fragile vessel. He had not floated the Deshka for several years, and he was not at all happy with its change in character as we headed for its juncture with the Little Susitna.

Midnight was approaching when a band of white water stretched like a silver streak across our path, and the echo of ripples indicated shallow water. Mike decided to wade ahead. Rain was still falling.

"Mike, what did you find?" the boys called to him as his long-legged form emerged in the darkness. "Heaven!" was his reply. For a marker, he had planted his paddle in the riverbed, and he had now returned to guide us to a grassy island large enough for only the big tent, which, with cold and wet fingers, we all fumbled to erect. Snuggled into dry down sleeping bags, the five of us fell into the deep sleep that rewards the intrepid explorer to whom bears and moose, at least for the moment, have become insignificant problems.

We awoke to more rain. Mike had planned to scramble eggs for breakfast, but our small island did not have a stick of firewood on it. Ham sandwiches made a fine breakfast. And what adventurer is not eager to strike out again with the lure of a new day ahead? We realized our night's good fortune when we paddled for almost two hours before the river again settled into a pattern of numerous gravel bars and we could stop for coffee.

During the afternoon we stopped to fish. I caught small grayling. But my husband's lure was snapped up by something big and furious; unbelievably, he had caught an early silver salmon on a fragile two-pound line! Mike and I ran behind him with all sorts of helpful advice as he played the thrashing creature downstream. His determination was to win the battle, mine to have salmon for dinner—although Mike's shouts and instructions indicated we'd have neither. My heart pounded as the big silver fish flashed away again and again, tiring, then reviving, hiding, and flipping. At last the battle ended. My husband proudly lifted the beautiful salmon ashore. Mike broiled the salmon fillets on a wooden stake surrounded by glowing coals and served them with fresh lemon slices, hash brown potatoes, and green peas, in addition to a rainbow trout that Matt had caught, wrapped in foil and tossed onto the coals. What a feast!

We could have traveled on the river happily for the rest of the summer, but the next day our pilot, Dave, would be coming to search for us at a prearranged spot near the junction of the Deshka and the Little Susitna rivers. So we set out for a small cabin Mike knew about. Skies were still gray, but the rain had ceased and the cabin came into view on the right bank just before dark. Established years before to shelter stranded hunters or casual travelers such as ourselves, the rustic building, long in need of repair, contained a camp stove, a gas lantern, pots and pans, and bunk beds from which the forest mice had pilfered nesting materials. Mike made immediate use of such grand facilities by stirring up a batch of pancakes for a bedtime snack. What mattered the sagging boards, the dusty littered floor, the creaky door? A party is a party!

On our last morning, I woke early and peered anxiously outside. The sky was blue and the sun was shining! There would be time to float and fish leisurely until Dave found us. Salmon leapt near the rafts, but they were busily working their way upstream to spawn and ignored us.

As we neared the river junction, we beached the rafts and unloaded the gear. Mike and my husband started inland to fish a small creek and the boys gathered firewood, while I waded around the bend downstream to try for a salmon. It was a day-dreaming kind of a day, so the black bear cub that bounced down onto the beach startled himself as well as me! After he scampered back into the woods, I stared for a few moments in anticipation of the appearance of an irate mother bear (I'd read about them). Then, upon analyzing my situation, without even bothering to reel in my line, I raced back to the boys on shore, where Matt, sitting comfortably near a small campfire, patiently untangled the dangling monofilaments, almost as if he didn't believe my story.

No fish were brought back by the returning fishing party. Just then, from the distant sky, came the droning of a plane. Dave dipped over our camp, flew off upstream, and turned to land in the soft spray of splashing pontoons.

It was good-bye again, as it been so many times from our many homes during our summer in Alaska. Good-bye, Mike. Good-bye, Dave. Without you, we could never have been intrepid explorers!

MY SISTER BEDA
June 1986

This is not a story just about Beda, as you will see later on, but let me tell you about her. We met in 1973 when my husband and I rented a bedroom in her small house in the Inuit village of Gambell on St. Lawrence Island in the Bering Sea, and we returned many times over the next ten years.

Beda was born in the village, grew up there, learned to read and write in the one-room schoolhouse, and finished her education at a state-supported high school on the mainland. Then she returned to Gambell, married Vernon Slwooko, the village's finest hunter and fisherman, adopted four children, and did not leave the island again.

Beda had learned all the skills necessary for survival in such an inhospitable land, where leaden skies and low clouds often concealed the high cliffs at one end of the island, while on the other side, angry seas pummeled the summer sand and winter's ice-covered beaches. To my way of thinking, Beda had lived a hard life. She had scraped and tanned sealskins, which she fashioned into hooded parkas, fur-trimmed boots, and bead-decorated wall hangings. She had strung fish and birds to dry on huge wooden racks and stored them for the winter's food supply. Grandchildren, tiny Jardine and Timmy, were always underfoot, as was the custom, because the villagers behave as a family and children are welcome in every home.

At midsummer Beda joined the other women and children in digging into the slightly melted permafrost to uncover artifacts—hunting tools, needles carved from walrus tusks, thread of braided sinew, and carved animals and birds—left by peoples of an earlier civilization who had lived in underground dwellings shored up by whale bones.

Beda was luckier than most of the women of the village, who lived in flimsy shacks constructed from debris blown onto the beach; driftwood from foreign shores; water-soaked planks from ships wrecked at sea; and large, strong whale bones. Jacques Cousteau had hired Vernon to be his guide during the filming of an Arctic Ocean diving adventure and had paid him handsomely. Vernon had wisely invested in real estate—several two-bedroom, rather deteriorated cement-walled cottages, built and inhabited by the United States Air Force during World War II. Vernon and Beda occupied one, and their son Timmy and his family lived in another. The third cottage was the only housing accommodation for visiting officials, museum directors, and the trader who arrived twice a year and purchased all the artifacts and ivory carvings that had been collected in the general store (one of the few sources of income for the villagers).

The derelict houses lacked plumbing and a water supply, but the sturdy walls withstood the blast of winter storms. Buckets of water for drinking and cooking were transported on sleds from a spring about a mile from the town. Water from melted snow was used for washing.

The island was allotted three whales each year, but luck had run out for several years. As I said, Vernon Slwooko was the finest hunter among the men of Gambell, so one year, just before our arrival, it was Vernon who caught a whale and towed the blubber-filled carcass to shore, where the villagers completely removed all the edible parts.

After I walked down to the beach to view the skeleton, I understood how the Inuit were able to support their underground dwellings with these strong bones. The enormous gray shell, which gave the impression of an artist's modernistic sculpture, was silhouetted against the sky. All around me were hills of well-polished stones, the colorful bodies of stranded sea urchins and scattered broken seashells. Across the ocean far from other human habitation, my evening vigil could have been in the Louvre or the Museum of Modern Art. I was in nature's art gallery.

Beda, a bit shorter than my five feet four inches, with short, wiry gray hair, skin wrinkled and weather-beaten from a lifetime of exposure to inclement weather, bore the stocky features of her race. Her dark eyes crinkled as she laughed at the antics of one of the children or greeted my arrival with a big smile.

During the years of our spring visits to Gambell, the modern world began to encroach. We attended the first graduating class of the new high school as four young people received their diplomas. No longer did the students have to leave their families and study for those four years in Nome. One late May we arrived in time to watch the erection of six windmills being built to furnish power to a laundrette. That year the snow and ice walls between the houses were so high that occasionally I became lost making my way around the usually familiar village.

Then came the telephones. Before that year, the islands' only form of communication with the mainland had been Vernon's two-way radio, as he daily reported the local weather conditions to the air controllers in Nome. The teenagers immediately took over the phones, and they chatted excitedly for hours.

Finally, of course, television arrived: a one-channel state-regulated program, which was available from noon until nine o'clock in the evening. In late afternoon I would stamp in from a day of hiking, slipping and sliding as if they were ball bearings on the small round stones that covered the land in and around the village, to find Beda settled in her broken-down sofa, her brown eyes staring uncomprehendingly at *As the World Turns*. We would smile at each other and I would join her, because at five o'clock came the live broadcast of the state legislature, much more interesting than the soap operas.

Our three-week sojourn always flew by too fast, and we had to leave the friendly village where the children shouted, "Hi, Grandpa!" when my husband walked by. "Good-bye, sister," said Beda, giving me a hug. "Good-bye, sister," I answered, and I gave Beda a big hug, pulled on my parka, and headed for the sand airstrip.

Our return route that year was via Kodiak Island, as we traveled down the coast on the Alaska state ferry. An Inuit couple came aboard. They stood apart at the rail on deck. No one spoke to them. So one day I approached, introduced myself, and told them I had just spent three weeks on St. Lawrence Island. The woman exclaimed, "That is where I grew up!"

I said, "Do you know Beda Slwooko?"

"She is my sister!"

Beda's sister had left Gambell and met and married her husband, who for twenty years had been the air traffic controller on Kodiak Island. They were on their way to their daughter's graduation from the University of Oregon. Beda's sister had lost contact with her family and now was eager to hear whatever news I could bring her.

So I told her everything I could remember about life on the island—the houses, the children, and grandchildren, the annual stipend for each family from the state's shared oil wealth, how every family now owned an ATV. We talked until the ferry eased into the dock at Prince Rupert, British Columbia, and we had to say farewell.

I could hardly wait to send Beda news of her long-lost sister!

ATTU REVISITED
1983

This Attuvian existence is so familiar, yet so indescribable, that it is difficult to write about it. On this, our fifth sojourn, my husband and I occupied a private room, the only ones so honored, as some rooms had six to eight bunks stacked floor to ceiling. Our room was about the size of a normal bathroom. The walls were of beaverboard, long ago painted blue, now cracked and folded, most of the paint having flaked off. There once had been a lavatory in the corner, but now only exposed rusty pipes remained, thrusting broken ends through the fragile wall. There were holes where light sockets used to be, three wooden wall studs where beaverboard had long since disintegrated, and peeling paint and plaster on the ceiling.

This was the luxury suite. There were two cots with thin mattresses, a shelf that a former occupant had made from an old metal bunk bed, and a makeshift wooden table somehow balanced on a four-legged metal base. There were lots of nails in the wall to hang our raincoats, caps, and jackets. We hacked apart a large cardboard box for carpeting, which almost covered the floor, adding warmth when we were dressing or undressing in freezing weather. We had a round kerosene heater, seldom used because of the annoying fumes. The whole abode was a wreck, but it was home.

Yet one of our friends, who had visited the island many times, walked in and exclaimed, "This is really nice!" and, looking at our see-through corner closet, said, "Oh, I really like that!" But she was lodged with five other people in an unheated bunkroom.

I thought I'd be stiff and sore after our first day in the field, but the next morning I felt great. Eli Elder and I had drawn the lot of pancake-makers for the duration—one hundred and fifty flapjacks to be ready before eight o'clock in the morning! After hiking and biking a dozen or so miles in one day, I told a new young friend that I was getting in condition to play eighteen holes of golf, my other hobby. At the age of sixty-two and pint-sized, my Viking genes had carried me through some long and arduous days in the Arctic.

One of our reasons for returning to Attu was to look for rare ducks, and we got them right away. *Pochards* were in the big lake the day of our arrival, and a few days later I was with a group that discovered a *falcated teal* bobbing in the waves close to shore. So already our trip was a success, though financially we had reached the point of diminishing returns. First-year campers added birds to their lists every time they went out exploring.

This season the roads were in better condition for bicycle riding than usual, but on the other hand, there was more snow. My new yellow Top-Siders were great. I could wear them comfortably the entire day, and I certainly could not get lost, as their bright color marked my travels over the rough road to Navy Town and beyond.

On our third day it rained a downpour. I had brought a big,

round jigsaw puzzle, picturing waterbirds of the world. Everybody worked on it and so passed the afternoon.

One day I made three bicycle trips of several miles each, then a ten-miler in the afternoon, the wind blowing so hard I had to push my bike the length of the airplane runway going out. But coming home, I never touched a pedal. Bicycling home with the wind at my back is one of my favorite memories of Attu Island.

Ducks: *pochard, falcated teal, garganey, snow,* and *tufted.*

And this year I finally got a *hawfinch*!

THE ATTUVIAN DIRGE,
OR THE LONGSPUR'S LAMENT

The Attuvians came in from outer space.
They came to run around this place
To search for birds not seen before.
But I'll be here forevermore,
    Squoke the longspur, "evermore."

They like the birds from other lands
With eyebrows, wingbars, stripes and bands.
My pretty collar they ignore.
But I'll be here forevermore,
    Squoke the longspur, "evermore."

They always look for larger things.
They pay no heed to my small wings.
But when the curlew leaves this shore
I'll be here forevermore,
    Squoke the longspur, "evermore."

When weather's bad they all complain.
You can't go birding in the rain.
And staying in is such a bore.
But I'll be here forevermore,
        Squoke the longspur, "evermore."

Mad men take the Temnac test
To view the eagle on her nest.
Why do they want to see it soar?
When I'll be here forevermore,
        Squoke the longspur, "evermore."

Each night the bird count is the same.
They just say "tick" when they call my name.
One of a kind they're waiting for.
But I'll be here forevermore,
        Squoke the longspur, "evermore."

It's lonely when they're gone, but then
They will all return again.
And I will meet them at the door
'Cause I'll be here forevermore,
        Squoke the longspur "evermore."

SONG OF THE CHORASNIAN FROM "CHRONICLES OF ATTUVIA"

The Reever is here, it's time to go.
Let me explain my tale of woe.

It started that day when the smew
Heard I was coming and flew.

The brambling would have been a prize
But it swished over the bluff before my eyes.

It wasn't so far to Massacre Bay
But the falcated teal had flown away.

When they discovered the tufted duck
I ran, but was just out of luck.

The black-tailed godwit was a beauty
But the bicycle repairman was off duty.

And the wagtail that turned up one week
Disappeared up Kingfisher Creek.

A bean goose in Henderson seemed strange.
When I arrived, he was out of range.

I biked to the ridge in a rush.
Saw only the tail of the eye-browed thrush.

And the snipe that I raced to reach
Had just escaped from Navytown beach.

They pointed to the eagle on high.
All I could see was blue, blue sky.

And the tattler with the gray tail
Just couldn't wait to set sail.

And the curlew with the long bill
Said "good-bye" from over the hill.

If I ever return, I have a new plan
That should have been clear when this business began.

I'll fly to Attuvia and then you will see
I'll sit in one spot and let the birds fly by me.

TO A SONG SPARROW

Song sparrow, song sparrow, flying high in the sky
Looking down on lakes and land
Do you see our searching band
    Plodding by?

Song sparrow, song sparrow, perching high on a pole
Merrily your song rings out
Telling all the world about
    Your gypsy soul.

Song sparrow, song sparrow, flitting along the bay
We were hoping for a shorebird
Your round brown shape is quite absurd
    Please fly away.

Song sparrow, song sparrow, squeaking in the grass
Are you only teasing us
Hoping that we'll make a fuss
    As we pass?

Song sparrow, song sparrow, sitting on a stone
We are quite aware of you
And all the things that you can view
	From your throne.

Song sparrow, song sparrow, rain doesn't daunt you
From nearby weeds your tinkly song
Cheers us as we walk along
	The whole day through.

Song sparrow, song sparrow, do you ever sleep?
When I waken from my dreams
From the darkened room it seems
	A night watch you keep.

Song sparrow, song sparrow, while we must return to the city
King of Attu you'll remain
Guarding with song your domain
	Sitting pretty.

PART III
CHRISTMAS

THE WALLCREEPER
December 2002

I stood in the little airport in Málaga, Spain, two days after Christmas, an e-ticket to Barcelona in my hand. I was on my way to search for a *wallcreeper*, a beautiful bird that breeds on sheer cliff faces at three to six thousand feet, where it gleans insects from the perpendicular walls of the high mountain ranges. The inaccessible sites are impossible to see from below. However, the *wallcreeper* is an altitudinal migrant, so in winter it descends to lower elevations to garner its meals in mountain foothills—in this case, the red rocks of Spain's Pyrenees range.

I don't remember where I learned of the Boletas Bird-watching Centre, which is located at the base of the Pyrenees Mountains in Loporzano, but probably from a Canadian birder friend who often travels to out-of-the-way birding spots on her own and passes information on to me. So in early autumn I had e-mailed Josele at the Centre and asked him if there would be an opportunity to find the *wallcreeper* during the Christmas holiday weeks I spend in Torremolinos.

"This is the only time of year we can find the bird," he messaged.

Next question: "Will you take me to find it?"

"Yes," came the reply. "Come to Barcelona, where I will meet you and drive you to my home."

I e-mailed him my credit card number to buy an air ticket for me, and the next day I printed out an e-ticket from Malaga to Barcelona for December 27.

In order to identify ourselves in the crowded Barcelona terminal, Josele and I both carried binoculars. After introductions, he pulled my small wheeled carry-on bag to his jeep in the parking lot, and we began the three-hour afternoon drive to the Centre.

Along the way we talked about birds, and when I confessed that a *green woodpecker* had eluded my many European searches, Josele smiled and said that we could find one—a bit out of the way, but not difficult. Thus, late in the day we saw several *green woodpeckers* in small roadside groves, the trees thinly scattered, making the birds easy to spot. Now, except for the *capercaillie* and the *wallcreeper*, I had seen all the nesting bird species of Europe and Britain.

Josele's home was a rambling stone structure, a reminder of the many thick-walled Moorish castles one sees on hills throughout the country. It was filled with warm carpets and deep, comfy chairs. A fire sparkled in the fireplace. His wife, who usually prepared meals for his clients, was away making a holiday visit to her mother, but Josele busied himself in the roomy kitchen, and soon we feasted on bowls of thick soup and chunks of hard-crusted bread. Tired from the long travel day, I snuggled under the fluffy down comforter and fell asleep.

After early morning coffee and croissants, Josele and I departed for an hour's drive to a canyon, where, from a bridge over a churning stream that splashed down from the mountain, we waited for a *wallcreeper* to appear. Though the morning sun was shining, the peaks created dark shadows against the rock face. The air was cool and brisk. But, disappointingly, no *wallcreepers*.

An hour went by. Then we drove to a tiny village, entered a tavern, and ordered coffee. Josele spoke to the tavern keeper, who apparently was knowledgeable about the *wallcreeper* sightings from the many birders who dropped in with their tales of success, or lack thereof.

On the road again, we drove to Josele's second-favorite *wallcreeper* site. Now the day had become comfortably warm, the sun shone into the crevasses, and within minutes we saw two beautiful *wallcreepers* fluttering against the red rocky pinnacle in front of us. We watched and watched, dazzled by the butterfly-like jerky flight and short glide of the birds that revealed the spectacular red, black, and white markings on the spread wings. In their constant motion, we could easily follow their busy gleanings.

I hated to leave, but we had a day of birding ahead of us, and my guide especially wanted me to see a *lammergeier*, an enormous, long-winged vulture of mountainous steppes, a bird I had seen only once before, at Zeus' Cave in the mountains of Greece. We identified many European bird species that day: *common finches, fieldfares, thrushes,* and *swallows,* and finally the *lammergeier* soared on windy thermals above us. What a day to remember!

Josele expected his wife to return the following day, and they had plans for more holiday visits, so he sent me back to Barcelona in a taxi. To my surprise and amusement, the driver was a golf fan and full of the details of the Portugal Open, then in progress. Hole by hole, he vividly described the rounds of the previous day, and that definitely shortened what would otherwise have been a monotonous trip to the airport.

I deplaned at Málaga and decided to catch the train back to Torremolinos. I found my way to an iron-railed catwalk from whence I descended by stairway to the ground level. There I encountered an automatic ticket machine, which, after I deposited a franc, emitted a ticket and allowed me to open a gate in the fence and cross over to the platform, where I waited for the train that comes along hourly.

I got off at the Torremolinos station, contentedly pulled my wheeled backpack over the uneven brick streets, and bumped down the eighty-three stone steps to the level of the sea, and I was home again.

The *wallcreeper* was my Christmas present to myself!

CHRISTMAS DOWN UNDER
December 1997

My husband and I had birded in Australia three times before spending a week of our 1996 Christmas holiday in our favorite corner of the continent: the northeast Atherton Tablelands.

Our first visit occurred in 1981 at the end of a thirty-six-day circumnavigation of Antarctica when the ship docked at Christ Church, New Zealand, and we continued on to Melbourne, Australia. A year earlier I had written to the Australian Ornithological Union, asking for help for two birders on their first attempt to find local bird species. Offers came from everywhere! So from You Yangs in the state of Victoria to O'Reilly's at Green Mountains in Queensland, our daily list of new birds accumulated almost faster than we could count them.

In 1989 we joined Philip Maher for an outback camping and birding tour—bumping along over narrow roads, pitching tents, dining around an open campfire, sleeping soundly. Thus we acquired such interesting species as *red-tailed cockatoo, chestnut-quilled rock pigeon,* and *Australian pratincole.*

Back again in 1993 for an invasion of the York Peninsula, guided by a young friend we met on the Cairns waterfront and chauffeured by his fifty-year-old friend who owned a four-by-four vehicle, which was necessary to maneuver in and out of the rut-filled dirt roads and sometimes rocks and chasms as we occasionally drove cross-country. Ranch crews had just abandoned their dormitories before the oncoming rainy season, and we had permission to use the sleeping lofts and enormous kitchen, where we cooked our food on an iron stove fueled by a wood fire. Quite an adventure.

Now it was 1997, and our wants were few. We had just finished a pelagic birding trip south of New Zealand, so we chose a perfect place for our Christmas holiday: Chambers Wildlife Rainforest Lodges, in the Atherton Tablelands, where, true to their promise, we found privacy, peace, and tranquility.

The Chambers' place, open-aired cottages, is set in 1,200 acres of tropical highland forest. A mile away is Lake Eacham, and easily accessible paved roads lead to Crater Lake, virgin rain forest, national forests, and wetlands.

On our arrival we found a neat, one-bedroom apartment set high on stilts. It had a fully equipped kitchen including a microwave, lots of hot water, maps, field guides, and, best of all, two walls of windows overlooking a rain forest so near one could almost reach out to touch the leaves on the trees.

We stored away the foodstuffs we had purchased at the supermarket on the way and settled down in our home away from home.

First we studied a map of our surroundings. One can drive on a scenic roadway cut through the forest. A mile-long circular walking trail gives a birder a choice of which direction to follow, making it possible to keep the sunlight behind. Another trail leads cross-country to Lake Meacham, a lake just large enough to circumvent on a morning's walk.

Without moving an inch from our front doorstep, we watched brush turkeys pecking about on our small lawn, and behind us spotted catbirds ventured through the open window into our kitchen, looking for a treat. But the walking trail, always a source of unexpected encounters, beckoned enticingly, and with a whole week ahead of us, we could saunter. *Spotted bowerbirds, Victoria riflebirds,* and *crimson rosellas* became common sightings, not to mention *Lewin's honeyeaters.* On our daily walks on the trail that began at our doorstep, we found fifty-seven species of birds!

A nice surprise was discovering that Glen Holmes, one of Australia's best-known birders, now lived in nearby Atherton. We had become friends with Glen and his artist wife, Ginny, when they lived near Binna Burra Mountain Lodge in southern Queensland. Glen owned a truck, and one evening he offered to drive us down the road, where we finally found a bird we had sought many times without success: a *lesser sooty owl.*

I'll never forget Christmas Day. We discovered that secretly we each had packed a gift for the other. I opened a small package to find a little gold box that, when opened, revealed a built-in watch. It was beautiful. My gift to my husband, more prosaic, was a golf shirt—yellow, his favorite color. The centerpiece at dinner was a single candle tucked into a heap of pinecones. How could we ever forget our rain forest apartment in the fresh mountain air surrounded by a forest chockablock full of colorful birds?

Did I say at the outset that the Chambers Wildlife Rainforest Lodges was the perfect place for our holiday? It was!

DINNER AT BRETT'S WHARF
December 1997

The day was Christmas Day, 1997, and my husband and I were sitting in a small, cheerless motel room somewhere near the Brisbane, Australia, airport. The view from our window looked down on a quiet, dusty street, where all the shops were closed and locked. We were tired after our busy week hiking birding trails, and we had slept late. I sat rather forlornly at the small desk, idly turning the pages of an information pamphlet describing the delights the city of Brisbane had to offer.

I came to the restaurant section and began to study it. The advertisements were alluring: "seafood," "Italiano," "smorgasbord."

But all were situated near the city center or in the suburbs. I found a city map. Only one restaurant was within walking distance of our motel, a mile away on the riverfront: Brett's Wharf.

We searched for clean clothes suitable for a holiday, which turned out to be a white shirt and khaki skirt for me, and a yellow golf shirt and khakis for my husband. By that time it was noon, and the walk was a long, hot one.

We opened the door to the restaurant, walked in, and gazed upon the largest dining room I have ever seen — and every table was filled with families in their Christmas finery. It had not occurred to us that we would need a reservation.

A hostess approached, and we asked if she might have a table for us. She smiled and answered, "If you had phoned for a reservation, we would have said no, as every table was booked for today. But we do have one empty table for two. The dinner cost is fifty-four dollars." We didn't bat our eyelashes, and we followed her through a maze of tables crowded with chattering guests. Grandparents, parents, children, and babies surrounded us, everybody smiling and happy.

Our waiter quickly discovered we were Americans. The maître d' had worked for a short time at a hotel in Florida. He strolled over to our table, which was covered with white linen, silver cutlery, and a vase with a single rose, and welcomed us.

The first course was turtle soup, which was followed by a wonderful salad, a fish course, and then a dinner plate heaped with thick slices of roast beef and vegetables. And I, who hardly ever eat dessert, could not resist the ice cream bombe covered with a caramel-chocolate-rum sauce and sprinkled with nuts and cherries. I ate the whole thing!

We lingered on the railed deck of Brett's Wharf, watching the gulls and terns circling over the water. Then, contentedly, we slowly walked back along the silent windswept street, extremely pleased with our fifty-sixth Christmas together.

PART IV

JOURNEYS

BIRDING ON THE MARCO POLO TRAIL
May 1992

I had a free ticket to anywhere in Europe—a reward for
flying on the last Pan Am flight to Nairobi, Kenya. After
studying various possibilities in birding travel brochures,
I decided that Russia and the Caucasus Mountains would offer
a new adventure and some interesting birds. So Birdquest, a
British tour company, and seven Brits got me, and London was
my destination.

At Heathrow Airport, British Airways was a turmoil of a
thousand people milling about at fifty different check-in coun-
ters, and I despaired of finding my people, until I spied a group
check-in sign, and there was my group actually waiting for me.
I sighed with relief.

We met Yelena, our guide—a version of Goldie Hawn, with
yellow hair, big eyes, and a big smile. At the Cosmos Hotel we
had a terrible dinner, but our group consumed four bottles of
champagne.

My alarm woke me at four-thirty in the morning for our flight
to Mineralnye Vody in the Caucasus Mountains, an alternate

destination, as we could not land in Tbilisi, Georgia, because of the fighting there.

Stavropol, Gorbachev's home, also a recreation area where mineral springs are used for curative purposes, was only two hundred and fifty kilometers away from Mineralnye Vody. In the distance were blossoming trees and snow-capped mountains.

We immediately began our bus ride to Teberdinsky Nature Reserve in Dombai and encountered our first village, which was a Cossack settlement. Our lodgings were an unheated ski lodge, and the noon meal was fatty chicken soup, chopped crab-like fish in a small casserole, bread, fried potatoes, and cold cabbage. I must insert here the information that I am a vegetarian, and you must be prepared for occasional comments about the food.

A walk in the woods produced my first new bird, a *green warbler*, and we returned to another awful meal: slices of cucumber, bread and cheese, hard-to-cut chicken (for all but for Chris, my vegetarian compatriot, and me), plus a small pile of overcooked peas.

A Key Lady on every floor kept the room keys while the hotel guests were out. Throughout the trip, every evening the kind women filled my pint thermos with boiling water that had been heated over the flame of a samovar.

I did not sleep well. Maybe it was jet leg. We departed at six in the morning with a bagged breakfast. Several pairs of *Caucasian black grouse* strutted around the hotel grounds, the males displaying their long, decurved tails. Then we were off for an afternoon in a nature reserve in Jamegad Valley: The day ended with hot water at bathtime and a nice bird list: *Cauasian snowcock, lesster spotted woodpecker, mountain chiffchaff,* and *red-fronted serin.*

Another early walk in an evergreen forest began shortly after my alarm rang at five. We ate lunch while resting on the grass beside a flowing river, and then all afternoon we walked uphill through rock piles we tried not to stumble over. We saw lots of migrating *red-throated pipits* and *yellow wagtails,* and a very good bird sighting was a *Krueper's nutchatch.*

The next day, after a predawn walk, we departed for a three-hour flight to Askabad, Turkmenistan. Here my lodging was a big spartan hotel, and happily we found *Turkestan tits* in the neighboring trees.

The next morning we drove to a mountain draw, where I walked all morning carrying my Kowa telescope. Aware of my five-foot-four frame and 107 pounds, at first the Brits were wary, fearing I might ask for help. But having carried a heavy Questar scope most of my birding life, the lightweight Kowa was no problem. After this, I never went anywhere without it. The day's bird list produced: *see-see partridge, streaked scrub warbler, Finsch's wheatear, desert finch,* and *Menetries's warbler.*

Perhaps I should take a moment to describe my mates. All were Brits. Steve Madge, our leader, has the sharpest eyes of anyone I have ever birded with, as you will later see for yourself. Chris is the other vegetarian, so we suffered together. Alan works all over the world for the Royal Society for the Protection of Birds. He is skinny and finished my dessert every day. Peter D. is an immigration officer, a big person, and often at dinner amused us with funny stories about trying to apprehend illegal immigrants. Peter C. wears a mustache and speaks with a clipped British accent. He is a professional with the British Natural History Museum and has collected skins in several countries. Tim is a photographer and has the world's best collection of Indian and Central Asian bird slides. His wife, Irene, a good birder, carried some of Tim's camera accessories instead of a scope. Stef, always with a smile, has a walrus mustache and reminded me of a British colonel. The Brits really do say "bloody" and "bloke."

I was happy the next day when we stopped at an outdoor native food market, where I tried to buy apples; only a local man, when he noticed the difficulty I was having trying to negotiate the transaction, presented me with two apples from the pailful he had just bought. Then I purchased and immediately ate fresh strawberries wrapped in a paper cone.

The ninth of May is a holiday for the Russians, marking the end of World War II. On our last day at Askabad we drove into the mountains and walked across many passes looking for a *pale rock sparrow*, which we did not find. Checking off our list of birds sent us off to a late bedtime: *rufous scrub robin, Savi's warbler,* and *barred warbler.*

The day after the holiday we visited a marsh before our airplane departure time and found *Blyth's reed warbler, paddy field* and *clamorous reed warblers,* and *blue-cheeked bee-eaters.* Then on to a picnic breakfast.

We arrived at Chardzhou, where after lunch we drove to the desert in hundred-degree weather and walked until dark in soft sand pocketed with occasional saxaul bushes. *Pander's ground jay, Uppcher's warbler,* and *saxaul sparrow* made this a grand day.

Out again at five o'clock. It had rained during the night, so the sand was firmer. We crossed many dunes in our search for a *desert sparrow,* which I had seen in Morocco, and we did find them. For a while I pleasantly scouted on my own and saw birds up close, especially the *ground jays.* At noon we drove to a museum, which was surrounded by trees full of migrant birds. In late afternoon we stopped along a riverbank and scoped for terns and waders. A *Penduline tit* was a new trip bird.

We were to take the train to Bukhara, Uzbekistan, but because of a broken bridge, our group had to pile out and transfer to a bus on the other side of the repair area. The afternoon sightseeing at mosques and bazaars was something different from the vigorous hiking of the previous days. I bought a silver bracelet and a small painting.

No sluggish birders today, as we left at five in the morning for a desert marsh. The heat was oppressive as we birded around the lake for several hours, then converged at the bus for lunch. A good new bird: *white-throated bush robin.*

It rained hard all during the next afternoon. Irene saw her life *smew,* so at dinnertime she ordered champagne, and then Steve ordered another.

We drove toward the foothills of the Tien Shan mountains. As we were trying to depart, the Key Lady interrogated us, shouting questions repeatedly, as if by repeating she would get the idea into our heads, which she finally did. I recognized the word *zavtra,* which means "tomorrow," and realized that she was asking if we would need the rooms the next day. So I was able to say *"sivawdny zdass da"* ("today, here, yes") and *"zavtra nyet"* ("tomorrow, no"). The usually stolid, dour woman was so pleased that she took our keys, grinned, and waved good-bye.

In the afternoon our bus broke down, so we hitchhiked into town with a passerby who was driving a small van. Then we visited the impressive observatory built long ago by Ulabek. New bird: *Yellow-breasted tit.*

May sixteenth, I woke up with a sore throat. But it was four o'clock and we had to leave for the airport for our flight to Tashkent. It rained most of the day, which it is not supposed to do in the desert, and I shouldn't have gone out with my fledgling cold, but I kept petty dry under my umbrella. I tried to send a fax home, but the machine was out of order.

This day was our most vigorous mountain climb of the tour. On some of the steepest inclines, steps had been packed out of mud and supported with wooden stakes. We passed an interesting cemetery with tombstones marking the graves of mountain climbers who had died. There were thousands of strips of white rags tied to the surrounding trees—prayers for the dead, I was told. After climbing through a pine forest, we finally broke out above the tree line onto a mountain meadow.

It was a beautiful day. And here Steve proved his expertise, when after hours of searching by all of us, he found a *Himalayan snowcock*, which made the mistake of blinking its eye, on the far side of the valley. We sat on rocks in the sunshine during our lunch break, and I thought how lucky I was to be in this particular place on this particular day. Our sightings of *azure tit, Evermann's redstart, black-throated accentor,* and *red-mantled finch* only added to my pleasure.

To me, making my way down a mountainside is always more difficult than climbing up. Still, we were back home early, so I made my only visit to the hard-currency bar and bought a can of cold beer.

Driving through flat country nearing the Tien Shan mountains, we arrived at Alma Ata, Kazakhstan, a city of nearly 3 million people. We climbed into three taxis to a dam to look for the rare *ibisbill,* which breeds only on rocky streambeds in the mountains of Asia and India. Eventually we gave up on that location and moved higher up the road, where we all stood staring down from a concrete abutment at the stone-strewn riverbed below. The stones did not move! Evening approached. Just when we were ready to give up, Chris spotted it! A beautiful male—white and black and red. Apparently, it had been resting, tucked in among the rocks in perfect camouflage. Luckily for us, the *ibisbill* became hungry and began to move. This was my target bird. I paid for wine and champagne at dinner.

Another long day began at four-thirty wake-up, as we were going north of the city to a desert habitat, the last known sightings of *yellow-eyed stock dove.* It was hot, and we walked all day

under the desert sun. In spite of the early start, I felt better
and had some energy again. Our day's ration was one slice of
bread, one egg, one small tomato, and a can of tinned fish. With
hot water from my faithful thermos, I had instant pea soup for
lunch. We found the regular *stock dove* at an overlook near a lake
surrounded by hills. On the way back we stopped at a tiny kiosk
for a fruit drink. I couldn't tell what it was, but it was cold, and
we all gulped down two servings.

I wasn't prepared for the next morning's drive to the mountains, because Steve had said "foothills," so I had worn only a
sweatshirt, and that wasn't enough for the cold, the wind, and
finally the rain. I trudged along miserably. Lunch was one chunk
of bread, two eggs, and two tomatoes. Then we walked several
hours up a road in a beautiful spruce forest, under snow-capped
mountains, where dwells the *blue-throated redstart*. Back at the
hotel, I sent a fax home to my husband, and this time it went
through.

Our flight to Tselinograd had a ten o'clock at night departure. On our arrival we were informed that our connection to
Moscow had been canceled and we would have to leave the following night.

So the next day we took a five-hour bus ride to a big lake,
and we did not get back until late, for our evening flight to
Moscow. Here we drove by some of the huge collective farms
with dozens of farm machines parked in long lines near ware-
houses. But it was a really good birding day: *black lark, white-
winged lark, black-winged pratincole,* and *white-headed duck.*

Our two o'clock in the morning arrival in Moscow found
me beat, and I needed sleep! So I slept while the others went
birding in Lenin Woods. When I finally awoke, I made a cup of
coffee, ate the fresh roll and cheese delivered to my room, took
a bath, and did my bird list. Did I feel guilty? No.

We spent the afternoon with Yelena on a tour of Red Square and the Kremlin, which we reached by riding the fabulous Metro. I had thought I didn't care about being a tourist in Russia, but its history and buildings, especially St. Basil's Cathedral, impressed me. We watched the changing of the guard at Lenin's tomb; the uniformed soldiers high-strutted along the square.

I was still to see a life bird on our last morning, at Moose Island. Steve took time to lead me into a little copse, where a *thrush nightingale* was singing, a bird the other birders had found the morning I slept in. So thanks again, Steve, for your wonderful eyesight and compassionate leadership.

At our farewell dinner party we all had to list our five favorite birds of the trip—a hilarious process, as obviously we all had different opinions about the rarity or beauty of a species. Safely back in London, I said good-bye to my companions, all of whom I now dearly loved.

And when my husband met my flight, he was holding an orange and a banana in each hand.

How was that for a happy ending!

FIJI ON PENNIES
January 1993

We hadn't planned to visit the Fiji islands with its thirty-one endemic bird species. Well, not really, although in the back of our minds was the possibility that, after our two-week camping trip in New Zealand, if our funds were not too low, we might stop there on our way home. After all, the stopover was free.

From a brochure of a travel agent in New Zealand, we chose a place to stay on each of four islands: Viti Levu, Vanua Levu, Taveuni, and Kadavu, each of which is home to endemic birds. We didn't have any information about how to look for birds on Fiji, but we had brought with us photocopies of color plates from Belcher's *Birds of Fiji in Colour*, a heavy, shiny-paged coffee table book.

From Auckland, we arrived at the airport in time for our evening flight to Nadi, on Viti Levu, to learn that our flight had been canceled! How awful to walk up to a check-in counter in an empty airport and read a flashing message on the screen: "Air Pacific regrets that Fl. #443 to Nadi has been canceled." We spent the night at Harbour View Motel on Auckland's coast. The next day the plane departed at noon. Fiji got a bad introduction because Air Pacific lost two of our bags.

It was late afternoon when we arrived at the Dominion International Hotel with its simple, clean rooms. On an evening walk we found our first endemics on the hotel grounds: a *wattled honeyeater* and *red-headed parrot finches*, and on top of a tree perched a *Fiji woodswallow*.

Ordinarily, one can drive the entire length of Viti Levu, the main island, from Nadi at one end to Suva, the capital, at the other, in about three hours. But a recent cyclone had destroyed the iron bridge that connected the two halves of the island at the village of Sigatoka. On reaching Sigatoka by bus, we found that every little boat owner was running a private ferry at a dollar a person, and they were zipping back and forth, often dangerously overloaded.

But the bus company had engaged a proper flat-bottomed ferry for its passengers. We came to the crossing in noontime's steaming heat, and the twenty-minute wait gave me just enough time to dart in and out of a few open-fronted shops to purchase a shirt to supplement my meager wardrobe. The only problem was that the shirt was olive-green with pink hibiscus and Polynesian natives printed all over it. Later it would be available to any of my friends needing a costume if invited to a luau.

A bus on the other shore was waiting to transfer us further on, but the driver had a manifest with the names of all passengers going to various resorts; so the afternoon waned as he checked every ferry arrival. The last passenger came on the four o'clock ferry after we had waited on the bus for three hours.

There was plenty to watch as streams of people walked by. Women climbed up the bank loaded with shopping bags full of food. Little girls were dressed for the Christmas holiday in lace-

trimmed frocks of pink and yellow, their jet-black hair in pony-
tails tied with colorful bows, absolutely beautiful. Hustlers were
making money while the emergency lasted. There were food
takeout stands, Coke and pop stands, and an ice cream vendor
from whom, in midafternoon, we bought ice cream cones.

We finally reached Sandy Point, three unpretentious little
cabins with housekeeping facilities. We carried with us bread,
peanut butter, jam, cheese, bananas, and oranges for breakfast
and lunches. But for dinner we found Angies, a small restaurant a ten-minute walk up the highway, with a dozen oilcloth-
covered metal tables. It was dark when we walked "home."

It rained our first morning, an oft-recurring event in the
islands; but our landlady had described a reachable bit of woods
on the other side of the highway. She told us to pass by the
Kula Bird Sanctuary, which contained only caged birds, and we
would find native bush.

A stream and woods with tangled undergrowth, a tall flowering tree with much bird activity, and a track that ran along the
edge of a grove of large trees offered a wild nature sanctuary.
We excitedly identified eight of our target species: *Fiji swiftlet,
orange-breasted honeyeater, Vanikoro broadbill, slaty flycatcher, Fiji goshawk, Fiji warbler, collared lory,* and *Fiji white-eyes.*

The next day grayish skies floated overhead with a few
intervals of sunshine. As we crossed the highway on an early
walk to the woods, a *Fiji goshawk* perched on a wire, and the first
bushes along the path produced a pair of *Fiji warblers* for excellent looks. It would have been nice to stay here an extra day, but
a taxi arrived shortly after noon to take us to Suva.

In Suva the Capricorn Hotel had been erected on a hill
in the center of the city, overlooking the harbor, a pool, and
gardens. Again we were strangers in a strange land, where we
were warned about our safety, especially walking alone into

forest bush. When he learned that we were going to go birding, our hotel manager, Mr. Gopal, said, "I will get you a dependable driver," and phoned a taxi driver to come for us early the next day.

Mr. Gopal was as good as his word, as our driver arrived early each morning and remained with us or picked us up later at an agreed place. We drove to Coco-i-Suva Forest National Park, but a sign at the entrance restricted entry until eight o'clock, so we slowly birded our way along the highway, where we would stop periodically to put up my scope. Thus we identified *yellow-breasted musk parrot* and *white-throated pigeons*.

Right on time, we entered the park headquarters office and met the head ranger, who, conscious of our vulnerability as tourists with binoculars and cameras, offered to walk the rugged trail with us. So began two days of exploring a really spectacular rain forest.

As is usual in the rain forest, one can walk for a long time without encountering a flock of birds. But when we reached the picnic area, almost at the end of the morning's walk, we found the flock! *Spotted fantail, Peale's pigeon, blue-crested broadbill, Layard's white-eye, lesser shrikebill,* and *starlings,* apparently all enjoying each other's company.

Leaving our friendly guide, after lunch I walked down to the FijiAir office, where I was informed that our flight to Taveuni had been fully booked and we were wait-listed! Behind the desk sat an agent, Uriah, who agreed to work on getting seats for us.

The next morning while waiting for the national park to open, we asked our driver to take us beyond the border of the city to a forest opposite a chicken processing plant (local knowledge), where we walked a narrow path into the adjoining woods and got caught in a morning shower, but were rewarded with a *lemon (golden) dove.*

Again the forest ranger walked with us, this time beginning at the picnic area, from where we slowly followed the sometimes precipitous track, closed in by damp, overhanging foliage, back toward the waterfall.

After lunch I returned to FijiAir and collected tickets to the other three islands. Friend Uriah had done it. Every ticket had been copied onto seven pieces of carbon paper. In the town museum finally we were able to buy a copy of *Birds of the Fiji Bush*, a true field guide.

I went shopping for something to wear. Near the hotel I found a small tailor shop with two women at sewing machines, ready-made garments hanging along the wall. I chose a cotton shirtwaist shift that they agreed to take in, shorten, insert a pocket, and have ready in an hour. The pattern was gray-green with blue-gray leaves scattered on a black background, and it is still one of my favorite summer dresses.

Our room contained a box radio that had a pretty good English station for music and evening news. From seven to seven-thirty each evening, *World News Tonight* was most interesting. But one night we were startled into laughing as the report ended with an announcement that the Buffalo Bills would play the Texas Rangers in the Super Bowl. This was our first news from the United States.

We were scheduled to fly to Taveuni at midmorning but were up at dawn anyway. It was lovely having breakfast on our outdoor balcony and watching the sun rise in the cool of the day.

We arrived at Garden Island Resort on Taveuni at noon. There, our hostess, Maureen, arranged for a driver to take us by jeep up Mt. Devereaux for an afternoon of birding. She also introduced us to Dr. Roy Ickes, a professor from Washington & Jefferson College, who was here with a group of students who were being exposed to a summer program of botany and natural history.

Roy was an ardent birder, so the three of us teamed up for the following day, which, luckily for us, meant sharing expenses. The jeep ride halfway up the mountain was over rough terrain. From the stopping point, we walked upward, and easily found two new birds: a *giant forest honeyeater* and an *orange dove,* which in the world is found only here, and when it flew we thought we were looking at a ball of flame.

It was unfortunate that we had wind and rain for most of the morning. When the mist cleared as the sun finally emerged, it was time for our ride back down. In the afternoon, Roy, my husband, and I climbed up a tree-dotted slope where robins and many *Polynesian trillers* filled the tree canopies.

Our last morning on Taveuni began with a very early morning ride to the gate of Mt. Devereaux. Nice morning, slight mist, and then sunshine. We found many entrances into the bush, but our flight was leaving at nine-thirty so we had no choice but to go back down and get a taxi to the airport. But along the way to our meeting with the jeep, an *island thrush* flew around us several times, and then alighted on a branch only ten feet away. And a spectacular end to our Taveuni visit was a *red shining parrot!*

At a small open shelter, we weighed in at the airport. Loading lots of cargo—sacks, rolled mats, boxes, and other things— held up our departure, but our itinerary included a two-hour stopover to connect to our Kadavu flight, so we weren't worried. But as our plane floated down and taxied onto the runway, we watched the Kadavu flight take off just as we were landing! Timetables are undependable in Fiji and planes are always being held for late connections, so this was inexcusable, especially as the flight took off with empty seats—ours!

The agent at the FijiAir desk went into the control room to

see if the flight could be recalled. He returned and announced that he could do nothing. I wish that I had had a tape recorder to follow the two-hour impasse that followed. They tried to send us to an island we had never heard of. All flights to Kadavu were fully booked until the end of January, which was repeated fifty times. We could return to Taveuni, but that wouldn't solve the Kadavu problem.

We suggested that they check with Sunflower Air, put us on their flight to Nadi and then on to Kadavu. Good idea, but that plane was full too. There was a flight to Savusavu at three-thirty (perilously near by now), so we suggested that we go there now and Kadavu later. "Fully booked." And now they decided that we would also have to pay extra for new tickets.

I was kind but firm and insisted that FijiAir must take care of us since the error was theirs. Finally, the chief agent, exhausted by my persistence, fetched Sammy, the operations officer. It wasn't his job to bail us out, but he felt bad about what he termed "mishandled passengers."

First he suggested our taking the ferry, which we said would be fine — until we were informed that the ship wouldn't sail until the next Monday evening. That wouldn't do. When he learned that we would take the Savusavu flight, which did have space in spite of former misinformation, he got on the phone with someone in control of things and obtained two spaces for us on the next Sunday's flight to Kadavu. By now, with the flight to Savusavu ready to depart, the agent was writing out the tickets by hand.

So, unexpectedly, we arrived at Kontiki Lodge, which was a super-elegant resort. On our arrival, we were greeted with cold drinks as we reclined in chaises on the patio. Hector MacDonald, a retired English rugby star, was the manager, and he was acquainted with everybody on the island, including Robin Mercer, the author of an early field guide to Fiji birds, and reached him by phone so we could ask where to find a *silktail*, our prime target bird. Robin gave us directions to the Herewa Peninsula.

The owner of the Kontiki, Tony Hoskins, was also in residence; that night we celebrated Hector's birthday with a fantastic luau. The only other guests were two honeymooning couples who didn't pay much attention to us old folks. After dinner, plans were made for a five o'clock taxi pickup in the morning to go to Herewa. We would take fruit and rolls along for breakfast.

We arose in the dark, dressed, and were ready the next morning, but no taxi, no fruit, and no rolls arrived. Now it was already too late in the day for our purposes. Instead, we spent the day exploring the magnificent Kontiki property, taking a trail to a waterfall after crossing a so-called golf course (an unmowed field dotted with dried cowpies and occasionally a tattered handkerchief tied to a stick, which we supposed was meant to be a green).

The walk to the rear of the parkland, which ran uphill into the forest, filled the morning. On our return, we sat for an hour in the sun under a ripe fig tree loaded with fruit and feeding birds, and there we had a sighting of possibly the most beautiful bird we'd ever seen—a *many-colored fruit dove*.

This time the taxi arrived on time, and we drove to the Herewa Peninsula with no early morning traffic along the narrow, one-lane road. During daytimes, the walking public swarmed along the roadsides. The instructions from Robin had been to bird along the mile between the ranch and the church at the end of the road—pretty specific, I'd say. As the morning progressed, families dressed in colorful finery passed us on their way to church.

Our last stop, almost at the entrance to the church, was at the base of a rock cliff. When I heard birds calling on the other side of the rocks, I climbed the wall by clutching at tree roots. I sat at the top looking into the copse and saw *golden whistlers, vanikos, shrikebills,* and others, and suddenly there was a *silktail,* white sides of tail flashing, almost at eye level.

Since we had to return to Kontiki by noon for the flight back to Suva, there wasn't time for further exploration, but we decided to return to Fiji soon to stay at the new developed bird sanctuary, in *silktail* habitat, which had been built by the Ornithological Society of New Zealand.

Again at the Capricorn came a friendly welcome from Mr. Gopal. It was Sunday and we had dinner at the only restaurant that was open, WangQ (very good).

We woke early for the flight to Kadavu, floating down onto the grassy strip of runway. Then we sat on a bench in hot sunshine and waited and waited and waited. Noon arrived. Finally, I walked to the nearby village, where I found a Fijian woman sitting on a bench outside the general store, holding two big bags of fresh bread on her lap. She was Mrs. Reece, our landlady!

A truck was supposed to appear to transport our luggage. No truck. Together, we started for the beach. A young man, Reece's diving instructor with no recent clients, and a young man from New Zealand, who with his girlfriend, Mickey, was camping in a tent at the resort, convened from some other part of the island. The boys carried my husband's suitcase and photography bag on the half-mile trek along a dirt road to the water's edge. The tide was low and our boatman was only a tiny dot wading beyond the surf to fetch the boat, which had been anchored at high tide earlier in the day.

We crossed the mudflats to a rocky beach where six women and several children waited, and we all had to wade in water almost to our knees to reach the boat. While we were waiting,

I put up my scope and found *Pacific golden plover, terek sandpiper, black duck, kingfishers,* and *white-fronted terns* at the edge of the surf in the distance.

It was midafternoon when we landed. After standing for a while unnoticed, when we asked about our accommodations a tall, husky-voiced women (man?) named Cyril pointed to a cabin at the top of a hill, slightly apart from a group of cabins along the waterfront. In the cabin there was only a bed! No other furniture of any kind.

We had brought flashlights, extra batteries, instant oatmeal, hearty soup mix, our own loaf of bread and a can of baked beans. We wouldn't have minded, but we had had the same kind of room in Costa Rica at Sabina's at Tortuguero National Park but for five dollars a day; so for fifty dollars a day, were we expecting too much?

When no offer of food came up from the kitchen, I walked down to the main building and told them that we were hungry. Someone made egg sandwiches, which were served with glasses of water. By the way, we never saw Mrs. Reece again!

The *Kadavu honeyeater* was easy to find around our cabin. Richard, the New Zealand camper, lent me his John le Carré anthology. I found *A Small Town in Germany* and read by flashlight until ten o'clock.

To find the proper habitat for the last two endemic birds, we would have to go by boat to mainland Kadavu. We were introduced to Seru, who would be our boatman.

We came down to breakfast, but no one was in the kitchen. We breakfasted on our oatmeal and canned baked beans. There was always a teakettle of boiling water on the kitchen stove. A very large woman came in and made sandwiches for us to take with us.

Seru did a good job of steering the little boat through choppy seas. He landed us in a sheltered lagoon and led us a short distance uphill to where his father and mother dwelled. Their cabin was small with only one chair, woven mats on the floor, and dozens of items that hung from the walls or on ropes or were stacked on shelves. They cooked outdoors on a wood fire.

From their sheltered homestead a track led up a steep hill, where we spent the morning. When we backtracked around noon, Charles, Seru's father, invited us into his cabin and served us fresh pineapple from his garden. He had been a policeman, then a Methodist preacher; now he was retired. He owned a shortwave radio, which he turned to music; then he engaged us in a discussion of world politics, a subject on which he was well informed. His departing gift to us was pineapples and papayas.

No one was up at five o'clock in the morning. I made toast on a round iron griddle on the stove. At six o'clock I sent Cyril to wake Seru. He appeared, groggy and sullen, and raced our boat so fast that we were drenched in spite of the shelter of our rain jackets.

Back at Charlie's I scouted the trail ahead, keeping trees and stones in line so I wouldn't get lost. Soon I discovered the track to the top, which had been blocked from my view by fallen tree trunks the day before. Within minutes I had a *Kadavu fantail*. I continued another half hour to the top, and while I stood there, a pair of *whistling doves* flew in! So golden, so beautiful!

Though the climb would be difficult, my husband decided to give it a try and was rewarded in minutes by a pair of *doves* feeding in the canopy. What a great finale to our Fiji adventure. In our two-week stay we had found all thirty-one endemics!

We returned to Charlie's for pineapple and a short visit. This time Seru's mother was at home, sitting cross-legged on a floor mat, sewing with a wheel-crank sewing machine, the kind I had used as a child to make doll clothes. She was stitching clothing for her grandchildren.

A storm came up suddenly, and it rained all afternoon. I finished the le Carré story.

I awoke in the night to sounds of surf crashing onto the beach below and bending the palm trees almost to the ground. I couldn't go back to sleep because I just knew we would never get off the island in the morning. The little planes could not fly in such a gale. The dirt runways would be a quagmire of deep mud.

But we did, even with no good-byes from the Reece's Resort staff. John, the boatman, carried my husband's suitcase and camera bag, and I wore my backpack as we hiked the mile to the open-shed airport. And just in time. We and our baggage had to be weighed, which would determine the number of passengers allowed on the flight.

Before the horrendous traffic mix-up, we had planned to make the luxurious Kontiki our last stop. So we tried to forget our forlorn departure from the Reece's Resort and remember Hector's warm farewell: "Come back soon."

We will!

BIRDING IN MADAGASCAR
September 1988

I t was April and the phone rang. My husband answered it, and I heard him say, "Yes, yes, yes." And that was that. He turned to me and announced, "That was Phoebe. She wants us to go to Madagascar in October."

Madagascar's land once was forested, home to many species of birds and mammals, but the forests have been decimated, cut and burned for subsistence farming, and only a few wooded pockets remain. The lemurs, those long-nosed, large-eyed animals unique to this island, are disappearing too; already they are restricted to a few national parks. We see them every day. Some are brown, some are beige, and some are a combination: browns, sifakas, ring-tailed, and the indri, which sets up an ungodly chorus that rings through the forest like a troop of lost souls. Some have long tails. Everywhere around us, they leap from tree to tree. Some are nocturnal, so we walked about at night with flashlights pointing randomly into the trees. One night we saw the tiny mouse lemur.

Our first birding experience was a campout in a dry forest

area. At Afrikansaka each person was issued a tiny tent, but somebody hadn't counted correctly, so the two of us had to squeeze into one. The only bathing facility was a big basin balanced on a fallen log. Suffering from jet lag and not sleeping well, everybody emerged from restless slumber at four-thirty in the morning to breakfast at a roadside café several miles away; then on to the walking trails, and it's always exciting when almost every new bird one sees is a new species.

The families of birds in Madagascar are so different from birds in the rest of the world. A *greater vasa*, a *red-capped coua*, and a *souimanga sunbird* were our introductions to the new terms that would become familiar later.

Here we found the *white-breasted mesite*, a long-billed, *pheasant*-like bird of forest and scrub. Fortunately, *mesites* call; even then, we had to lower ourselves into an almost prone position to watch them forage for insects and seeds. This habitat also produced a *rufous vanga*, a *crested coua*, a *Van Dam's vanga*, and a *cuckoo-roller*. Much excitement.

Our next destination was Perinet Nature Reserve. Delays are expected in third-world countries, so a day-long wait for a flight that was supposed to depart at ten o'clock in the morning kept us waiting in a dilapidated airport until seven o'clock at night! Luckily, on our arrival in the airport at Tana, the capital, I had purchased an excellent book by Tom Clancy. Even then, the wait seemed interminable. To facilitate group travel, on our three-day excursions to different reserves we left our big bags at the hotel in Tana and restocked whatever was necessary in a small pack. That works well, as shorts in camp and while hiking are the uniform of the day.

At Perinet we had a sink in our room. The hotel was situated over a railroad station that contained a restaurant. The train stopped here every day on its way to the coast and the passengers got off to dine. One night the lights went out and dinner was served by candlelight with candles stuck into empty wine bottles.

To reach Perinet, our transfer from Tana was a long drive through villages and rice fields and past fish and vegetable stands and many, many natives who thronged the verges of the road. In spite of our late arrival, an evening walk around fish ponds continued onto an uphill path to the top of a wooded levee until dark; suddenly, we needed our small flashlights to find our way home in this unexplored territory.

A misty morning at Perinet was followed by a misty rain for the rest of the day. So our bird list that evening contained a surprising number of new endemics: *lesser vasa, blue coua, wattled asity, Chabert's vanga, red-tailed vanga, short-billed tetraka,* and *kinkimavo.*

The next morning sunshine followed a six o'clock shower. All morning we tramped along narrow trails, peering in all directions for a *crested ibis.* An afternoon drive to a higher elevation ended in a quarry, where our leader got a life bird, a *Pollen's vanga,* and that was enough for everybody to celebrate.

With connections to Tana and on to Port Dauphin, a day of zigzag travel brought our group to the finest accommodations of the entire tour. Realizing that this would be our only free afternoon, we walked to the beach and waded in the ocean.

Then a very adventurous day was had by all. A morning drive over very bad roads and wandering sand trails, grass, bushes, and small streams with stick bridges (the bus was unloaded for these crossings) ended in our being paddled by local natives over a lagoon to an island covered with hills and forest. The big surprise was a catered lunch prepared by the chef at our hotel: charcoaled shrimp kabobs, a salad platter, zebu slices and veggies, fruit for dessert, and coffee, which was spread on a white tablecloth on the sand and devoured with delight. We had expected only an overnight at Port Dauphin, so exploring inland had been a bonus.

Thus we proceeded to the famous Berenty Reserve, the one most viewed on television, with its ghostly forest of misshapen trees, birding stops along the way. Our individual cabins were built on the reserve so that our lodgings lead right onto the trails. Here is what is called "gallery forest" (river lined with trees). Our camp was in dense jungle totally surrounded by plant life, including many orchids. Ring-tailed lemurs were common, and they expected to be fed bananas. Berenty is the best place to listen for the "song of the indri." *Giant coua, hook-billed vanga* on a nest, *stripe-throated jery,* and *gray-headed lovebird* were happily added to our bird lists that evening.

A very different dry habitat with strange trees filled the Spiny Forest, where on an early morning bird walk we found *kiritika* and *Madagascar hawk owl.*

Our last campout was on the west coast, which was dry and completely sandy, except for some small scrub-like trees and baobobs. These long morning walks at Mora Mora were in very hot weather, so at noon, lunch and a siesta were welcome. *Running couas* reminded us of our own western *roadrunner. Vangas* came in all sizes and colors, and the *brown mesite* lived here.

One day we encountered a newly built canoe, which had been fashioned out of a whole baobob tree. The natives first shaped the outside with hatchets, and then hollowed it out. Since the canoes are primitive and unbalanced, when men go out to sea they add a crude outrigger.

The natives dwell in very small bamboo-laced shacks. Their outdoor worktables are constructed of lashed sticks, the kind we built at Girl Scout camp and thought it was fun. The Tulear area is so dry now that local people dig holes to reach water for washing clothes and carry a supply of drinking water home in pails. The women carry everything on their heads in deep woven baskets.

At one time Madagascar exported a large part of the world's supply of sisal, but not anymore. The countryside is covered with rice paddies and a few vegetable plots. There is an Asian cast to the cities, where brightly painted red-and-blue rickshaws are pedaled along the streets. But we saw no bicycles which had predominated the city streets of China and elsewhere in Asia. If you saw a boy on a bike, his father was probably a government official.

All of Madagascar's wildlife is endangered, so the World Wildlife Fund sends specialists who are trying to preserve the endemic plants and birds. The struggle is without much cooperation from the government because there is no money for this purpose. Yet I believe the lemurs and birds will continue to exist as long as the reserves for them are under the supervision of the dedicated caretakers we met.

This totally unplanned expedition onto the island of strange birds and plants that was torn off the coast of Africa so many millions of years ago brought me a new understanding of the diversity of life on our planet.

I am glad my husband said, "Yes, yes, yes."

SOUTH AFRICA: SANI PASS
October 1994

If I could choose one outstanding experience during a
month-long birding trip to South Africa, I'd have no hesita-
tion in saying, "Sani Pass."

Sani Pass is in the high Drakensberg—a mountainous won-
derland with awe-inspiring basalt cliffs, lush yellowwood forests, and cascading waterfalls—which links the South African
province of KwaZulu-Natal to the independent kingdom of
Lesotho. Originally a rough mule trail until the 1950s, Sani Pass
is now a reasonable dirt road all the way to the top; four-by-four
vehicles are recommended. The tight zigzagging curves on the
road up to the pass ascend through sheer cliffs on a route known
as the Roof of Africa. Thousands of rock paintings depicting the
life of bushmen abound on rock faces.

Underberg, a village at the foot of the mountains, was the
home of Robin Guy, our guide. The tall, white-haired, energetic
gentleman immediately won our friendship by inviting us into
his garden for afternoon tea. Robin drives the challenging route
up to the pass several times each week and is the acknowledged

expert on the birdlife in this region. He told us, "While birders from elsewhere arrive looking for national 'specials,' I have an advantage over other birders simply by virtue of local knowledge, which adds enjoyment to the thrill of sharing 'firsts.'" We will follow in his footsteps.

Even though the day was waning, our tireless host insisted on a trip into the country to "get one new bird for the day." The extra hours were well spent, as a *Stanley's bustard* in full breeding plumage strutted around in the grass. A *red-winged francolin* flushed in a weedy field. Were we allowed to relax? Nope. An evening drive to look for a *cape eagle owl* perched on a wire at dusk proved that we couldn't always be lucky.

Most travelers make the trip to Sani Pass a day trip, having to return before the border at Lesotho closes at four o'clock. But the next morning, Robin's van, with the top rolled back, transported us over the notorious rocky, bumpy road to Sani Top Chalet for an overnight campout. "Bring windcheaters," he had advised.

At our first roadside stop, *cape rock thrushes* perched among the boulders. A *Drakensberg siskin* flushed from a roadside cutting. We stopped to show passports to Lesotho border guards. Another stop produced *buff-streaked chats* and *thick-billed larks*. At our third stop, in a protea grove, we found our first *sugarbird*, *Gurney's sugarbird*, a species high on our priority list. It is one of only two bird families restricted to South Africa; the other family is the *rockjumpers*. *Gurney's sugarbirds* birds have long, decurved bills, typical of nectar feeders, and long tail feathers. They depend on the blossoms of the protea scrub for food. We excitedly observed them climbing on the sturdy plant stems.

We reached Sani Top Chalet, a lodge situated on the very rim of the escarpment (nearly ten thousand feet above sea level), containing eight bedrooms, twenty-six beds, and a notice that water pipes are never frozen solid in summer, and dropped off our overnight gear. Robin had brought all the food we would need, and it was time for lunch.

Even though the wind blew briskly, we picnicked on an outdoor bench. As we ate our sandwiches and apple wedges, *orange-breasted (Drakensberg) rockjumpers* fearlessly approached. These are small birds with mostly brown-and-red plumage and long, white-tipped black tails. Seldom flying, they spend most of their lives running and jumping among rocks and grasses while hunting insects. Their scampering amused us but also made us realize how fortunate we were to be on this special mountain.

Our afternoon travels took us to the top of the mountain, where the atmosphere at this altitude was extraordinarily clear and bright. Rarely had I been driven on a road with so many hairpin turns. Here the tropical high-altitude scrubland produced the *bush blackcap*, listed as near-threatened. More rewards were *fairy flycatcher, southern gray tit, sickle-winged chat,* and a sighting of a bird we'd had only a small hope of spotting: the *cape vulture,* dark brown except for pale wing coverts, entirely dependent for food upon the larger animals. They are threatened with secondary poisoning as farmers put out poisoned carcasses to catch mountain predators. The *vultures* are declining at an alarming rate. We were lucky.

The night was cold. Back at the lodge, our only heat was from a fireplace in the main room, where Robin served us a hot dinner. So to our bunks with lots of blankets and my feet wrapped in my down vest.

Coffee at four o'clock the next morning, the stars still twinkling when we took off in our topless vehicle in search of a *mountain pipit.* It was cold, cold, cold, and windy as we drove across acres of grassland in search of the little bird. But if he was hiding in the grass, he did not show himself. We stumbled back into the chalet for the warmth of the fireplace and Robin's pancake breakfast.

We began our return journey on foot with a slow walk down the road until Robin picked us up. Our lunch stop was along a small, rocky stream, where *paradise whydahs* flaunted their long tails. And a late-afternoon search in Bulwer Woods produced the hoped-for *knysna loerie,* which, unbelievably, sat out in the open for five minutes. A *plum-colored starling* was the last find of the day.

The Drakensberg contains 290 species of birds on hiking routes on both upper and lower slopes of the mountains. Our short visit created memories we'd never forget. Some other interesting places in South Africa left us with memories too — Weaver's Nest, Hilltop Camp, Augrabe Falls, Klippe River Homestead — but Sani Pass outdid them all. Fantastic!

BIRDLIFE IN TROLLHEIMEN, NORWAY
July 1970

The beautiful country of Norway has attracted our family to spend two long summers there. The memory of a week-long walk through Sylene, staying overnight at the Trondheim Turistforening's lodges at Stordal, Storerikvollen, Nedalshytta, and Stugudal, probably more than any other thing, lured us back for a second visit.

Ten years before, our Norwegian cousins had planned our hiking vacation for us. This time, we bent our heads over the map of Trollheimen because my husband and I were intent on looking for birds in that region. We had read an extensive article about birdlife near Gjevilvatnet in the 1957 Yearbook and we had already spent six weeks photographing birds in Norway. Their Norwegian bird names were becoming familiar.

Our walk began from Grindal to Jodalshytta on a sunny July day. The wide road eventually became a narrow, rocky mountainside path. *Willow warblers* sang from thick woods, the *redwing* slipped quietly from tree to tree, flashing the bright red under his wings, and during our first lunch stop, down in a ravine below us, an *orange-breasted brambling* buzzed. Late in the afternoon, as we passed a large saeter (an upland pasture), *white wagtails* flicked their tails from a thatched roof; *meadow pipits* fluttered up in the meadow; *swallows* darted to and fro.

It was early evening when we finally circled the end of the lake and trudged thankfully into Jodalshytta, fortunately with the table set for dinner. We ate meatballs and potatoes as if we would never see food again.

Our first surprise on setting out the next morning for Trollheimshytta over "Goat Pass" was a *bluethroat,* his bright blue-and-red throat quivering as he sang his tinkly, metallic tune. A few minutes later a *golden plover,* outlined against the brown grass, announced his presence by repeating his plaintive call. The *wagtails* and *pipits* were our constant companions. At noon, settling down by a log bridge over a rushing river to eat lunch and watch for a *dipper,* which surely would live in such cascading water, not a *dipper,* but a *ring ouzel,* showing his white crescent, flashed by on his way upstream.

After reaching a fork in the trail, a steep ascent brought us quickly to higher ground on our climb to Goat Pass. Clouds blotted out the sun, and the wind began to blow, but in our eagerness to reach the top, we pressed on. Instead of following the ledge of the glacier-formed valley, our route would entail a climb directly up the mountain trail. Our heads bent into the violently blowing wind, which occasionally blew away the mist around us and the winding stream at the bottom of the valley became visible. "No birds up here," was our estimate of the situation. We were wrong: a flock of *snow buntings* landed before us on a patch of snow during our afternoon coffee break.

It seemed that we had been climbing forever. Beside us were fields of snow, little lakes of blue and turquoise, and black boulders everywhere, challenging our courage to jump from one to another while water thundered underneath. While we rested, two *ravens* flew overhead. A *cuckoo* called from a distant forest. At last the trail pointed downward again, but our motions were slow on the crooked, rock-strewn path. The *wheatear,* perched on a rock silhouetted against the gray sky, was almost missed.

Trollheimshytta was our home for an extra day. Baby *great tits* lived in a nest under our window; the yellow, gray, and black parents alighted repeatedly on the clothesline before proceeding to the nest with food. *Blue tits* flitted in the trees surrounding the hostel yard, while *black-and-white flycatchers* fed young in several old nest boxes.

The next day, even rain could not deter us from starting back to Jodalshytta, this time through Svartedalen. Along the sandy banks of the river ran *common sandpipers,* teetering and piping. The trail was an easy walk. One of the highlights of the trip was the sight of *reed buntings* feeding babies.

So far, the *dipper* had eluded us; but we give it one more chance. Gjevilvasshytta was our goal on the fifth day. Instead of the chipping of big *woodpeckers* in the birch forest, the only sound was the tinkling of bells of the goatherds. But *redpolls* posed on the fenceposts near the road leading to the cottage. On an evening walk, a *middle-spotted woodpecker* swooped into our sight and alighted with its characteristic shape against a large tree trunk.

Immediately after breakfast on our last day near the fast-moving mountain stream, the flower-bordered banks almost hid the repeated movements on a gray rock. A baby *dipper* bounced and bounced on his sturdy feet, right before our eyes! Soon we heard the warning call of the parent as the mother *dipper* emerged from the high walls of the canyon. She saw us and swerved away up the waterfall. Cautiously we followed; one by one we discovered the rest of the family — three more bouncing *dipper* children, bravely working their way upstream, attempting to find food in the rushing water. On and off all day we returned to watch the never-tiring spectacle of this unusual bird rearing its young.

Our day with the *dipper* family was a surprising and fitting climax to our mountain "birding holiday."

THE AMAZON IN PERU
January 1984

W ho has not dreamed of sailing down the Amazon, where monkeys swing through the jungle trees, parrots raucously shriek overhead, and piranha lurk in shallow waters?

My husband and I did just that, and the picture is quite true, although the Amazon is a very wide river, and only its tributaries are narrow enough to provide an arched roof of impenetrable forest leaves.

Palm thatch roofed the transport canoe that carried us in five hours from Iquitos, Peru's largest inland city, to Explorama Lodge, a group of little cabins built on a bluff in a small clearing along the Tambopata River near the Amazon's headwaters. No docks eased our embarking. Shouldering backpacks, we slid down the muddy riverbank and struggled onto the little vessel.

At first the canoe kept close to shore. Bamboo huts, dugout canoes, children playing, women washing clothes at the water's edge—all the activities of an Indian civilization passed before us. The coxswain perched high on the bow and kept an eye out for floating logs. Sometimes the Amazon was so wide we could hardly see the opposite shore.

Nearing our inlet, again precariously juggling our backpacks, we had to abandon the big canoe for a smaller one that carried us up a narrow winding channel to the Explorama Lodge dock.

Tucked into the jungle, set on stilts and connected by thatch-covered walkways, rooms had been constructed of thin slats. Each room contained a cot with mosquito netting, a basin, and a water pitcher. A set of written instructions on the wall directed us, "Pull curtain and throw wash water out the window, being careful no one is passing underneath!"

Too excited to unpack, and even though afternoon is not the optimum time for birding, we immediately investigated the first of many jungle trails that were to become very familiar. Almost at once our first new bird appeared in a tree within sight of the cabins: a *speckled spinetail*. Our group of birders filed quietly along the cool, shaded pathway that turned and twisted until it wound up in a high forest, where our reward was a *scale-backed antbird*, the first of more than thirty species of *antbirds* we were to identify. At dinnertime we served ourselves from a buffet that offered fish, rice, and many kinds of vegetables and fruit.

Had not the day been long enough? Did anybody want to go owling? Of course we did. Stars twinkled in the black sky, fireflies flashed their tiny lights all around, and only the soft shadows of our comrades betrayed our invasion of the dark forest. As our little group clustered together in anticipation, our guide played a tape of the call of the *crested owl*. Soon came a soft answer, then a whirring flight of feathers, and a giant shape landed on a tree limb high above us. The *owl* had enormous ear-like tufts, clearly displayed in the light of our beacons. Our first day in the jungle had come to a spectacular close!

Life on the Amazon fell into a pattern. Breakfast was at five o'clock, the magic time of day when life in the jungle begins to stir, birds begin to chatter, and cool air invigorates. The daily search for new neotropical bird species led us through the river's floodplain, an area of special kinds of plants and birdlife, up to the high forest, where, in an opening against the sky, treetops heavy with fruit attracted brilliantly colored *tanagers*: fourteen species, among them *green-and-gold, paradise, turquoise,* and *opal-crowned. White-eyed* and *maroon-tailed parakeets* as well as *blue-winged* and *dusky-billed parrotlets* squawked across the sky. Add to that a raucous *orange-winged parrot.* A *spangled cotinga* reflected the morning's gold sunshine. *Toucans* snapped their tremendous bills. And always we listened for calls of the wary *antbirds, antwrens,* and *antpittas.*

Just as we began to really feel at home, it was time to climb back into the canoes for a trip further up the Amazon to the Napo River. At the confluence of these two rivers begins the Amazon's three-thousand mile run to the Atlantic Ocean.

ExplorNapo Lodge, merely an open veranda built on stilts, became our new home. Our beds were mattresses placed in rows on the floor, each enclosed with a rectangle of mosquito netting suspended from the overhead. Chairs had been carved from logs and surrounded the long wooden table. Stairs cut out of tree trunks provided precarious footing for the journey from the lodge to the restrooms at ground level. But we loved it.

There was coffee and bread and jam to eat at dawn. There were morning hours on jungle trails, canoe rides to river islands, and afternoon walks to the shore, after the careful crossing of a bridge that had been built of logs laid side by side. We identified more than one hundred new bird species, from the tiny *sapphire-spangled emerald, white-chinned sapphire, golden-tailed sapphire,* and *blue-tailed emerald,* among eighteen *hummingbird* species; to the disheveled, helter-skelter *hoatzins*. But one of the best sightings was a *lanceolated monklet,* discovered by my husband, after everybody else had passed it by. Fortunately, *monklets* stay put for a long, long time.

Our delightful three weeks on the Amazon came to an end, and we reboarded the big canoe. Small clearings, thatched-roof huts, children waving from shore, clumps of mud sliding into the waterways, crecopias and vine tangles—all were treasured glimpses of the passing scenery.

We had fallen in love with this part of the world, so remote from our civilization, that we knew we'd come back—and we did!

PERU: FROM COAST TO MOUNTAINTOP
January 1984

As we drove along the coast of Peru, I knew what desert meant—brown, brown, brown. Rocks and sand. Hot at noon and cold at night. On ascending the Andean foothills, it amazed me that any roads had been built here at all. There were no superhighways, and I remember only twice driving on paved roads: the Pan-American Highway from Lima to Paracas and the road connecting Cuzco to Urubamba. Yet there were roads over the Andes connecting the entirely different eastern and western cultures. The distance from Puerto Maldonado to Cuzco took forty-five minutes by plane, but three days to drive in a vehicle.

We scoped the Paracas shoreline, and our rewards were *flamingos, grebes, cormorants,* and *boobies.* A fast motorboat took us out to the rocks and caves offshore, the famous guano rocks that are a major source of Peru's income as the guano deposits are mined and used in fertilizers. Masses of colorful *Inca terns, red-footed cormorants,* and a few *Humboldt* penguins inhabit the bare islands.

We found old Peru in the mountains above Arequipa. Here the peasants dwelled in villages of adobe huts and daily worked their small plots of land, sometimes terraced as high as the mountain itself. Their garments were heavy wool ponchos, large-brimmed hats, protection in all kinds of weather. The children, even the very young ones, shepherded the family's precious possessions: cows, sheep, goats, and llamas. Colorful woven sweaters, caps, and socks brightened the market squares. Infants stared solemnly with big black eyes.

The only relief from miles of desert were the occasional small canyons that supported a few shrubs and trees. It was interesting to start walking where there was no apparent sign of life, then surprise a *canastero*, a *miner*, or a *sierra-finch*. Sometimes the birds curiously popped up in plain sight; more often they flicked away behind rocks. Their very coloring was of the desert—browns, rusts, and tans. Glimpsed along a desolate roadside one morning, hummingbirds hovered: *sparkling violetear, black metaltail,* and *Andean hillstar.*

The beauty of jagged snowcapped mountains surrounded us at fourteen thousand feet. Finally we reached Lake Salinas. Upon leaving the van, we moved very slowly in the rarefied atmosphere. *Flamingos, Andean geese, avocets, lapwings, crested ducks,* and a *gray-breasted seedsnipe* were the specialties at this altitude. Ever-present *rufous-backed negritos* hopped among the rocks. It was an ideal spot for our picnic of cold chicken, cheese sandwiches, hard-boiled eggs, bananas, and mangoes.

The bumpy ride back down the twisting, turning cutbacks, sometimes half-blocked by a recent descent of great rocks, nevertheless was breathtaking. The gold-brown wavy sand dunes flowed around us. How many eons of erosion and wind had passed to create this magnificent view!

A few years later, the BBC series *The Flight of the Condor* carried us back to the land we had barely touched, but loved. How glad we were to have visited the majestic mountains of Peru!

A SAHARAN SUNRISE
January 1990

I was standing on the top row of sand dunes on the fringe of the Sahara Desert, beyond the red-bricked village of Merzouga in southern Morocco. It was January. It was dawn.

In all directions my eye encountered waves of sand. In the east, as the pink flush of the approaching day spread slowly above the edge of the world, shadows carved sharp, dark ridges that broke the monotony of the landscape. With my large-lens Questar telescope I circled the pyramid of sand and extended my view into the far distance, where a tiny lone camel rider, moving with an ungainly gait, plodded along. Occasionally, clumps of dry grass stalks clung to life, creating a pattern in the light of the brilliant sky that suddenly burst from the underworld. The world was breathtakingly warm and beautiful.

I thought, *This is the largest desert in the world, with its parched, forbidding land that took shape over thousands of years.* I tried to picture the caravan drivers slowly guiding their dromedary camels, the favorite animals used by nomads, from one oasis to another—wet rest stops, without which desert crossings by humans and animals would be almost impossible. In the distance, at the edge of this expanse of golden hills, I could see palm and acacia, which people in this desert have lived near ever since the Ice Age.

Before dawn, we, twelve birders with one desire—to greet the day from the highest peak—trod the sandy path from the village and began to climb. My heavy scope, carried by a shoulder strap clipped to a steel D-clamp on the tripod, rode on my hip. The distance to the top had not looked far, but on arriving at the summit of the first dune, another loomed before us, and after that, many more seemingly endless dunes.

Now stragglers gave up and returned to Merzouga. Fewer and fewer climbers continued to struggle in the soft sand, boots sinking into deep footprints, every step an effort. Was I discouraged? Yes, but somehow I managed to put one foot in front of the other, slower now, knowing the end must be near. Finally, it was. Five of our group had reached the top.

These moments, watching the sun rise and daylight spread out over the Sahara, were the highlight of my month-long birding trip to Morocco.

We were ready to return when, seemingly out of nowhere, a tall, dark-skinned Arab leading two camels, a big one and a small one, approached and asked if I would like a ride down. At first I shook my head, but then I looked at the faraway village, shimmering in the haze of the morning's rising heat. The cost? He raised five fingers. Five dirhams, or approximately fifty cents. I agreed.

The clad-in-rags Bedouin pressed the small camel (unwilling and with a great protesting roar) to the ground. No saddle. No reins. No stirrups. Just a flat board covered with a woven shawl for me to sit on!

The young camel first extended his hind legs, almost tossing me off. After he arose and began a bumpity gait, some time elapsed before I dared look around and view the countryside from my high mount. Even a young camel is very tall! The extended landscape, in the brilliant light of the new day, sparkled with sand, sand, and more sand.

My guide, leading his camels and carrying my scope, spoke to me in French and told me he had five children at home. I thought about how hard he had to work to make a living. We reached the village where our friends were waiting, and I gave the driver whatever Moroccan money I had in my pocket. He bowed over and over. I think this was a good day's job for him.

It was time for breakfast, and perched on the village's uneven adobe walls that enclosed the outdoor dining patio, we found *Moussier's redstart* and *Tristram's warbler*. It was a very good day's work for me, too.

PART V
REFLECTIONS

IN MEMORIAM — RTP

Only a few personalities are famous enough to be known by their initials: John F. Kennedy (JFK), Franklin Delano Roosevelt (FDR) — and forever a grateful nation will remember the big, gentle man who loved birds, Roger Tory Peterson, as RTP.

Painter, writer, student, teacher, his hawk-like concentration was amazing and his memory unbelievable, while his sharp facial features and locks of hair over a high brow made him a recognizable figure. His guide to the birds of North America introduced a new concept in bird identification and became a bible to watchers in the field.

My introduction to his fantastic memory came when, with a small group of birders on a tour to Greece, we were listening to what I hoped would be a *nightingale,* a bird I'd never seen before, singing and hiding in a small bush. Roger walked up and said, "That is not a *nightingale.* That is a *Sardinian warbler* imitating a *nightingale.* I heard that twelve years ago in Spain." Sure enough, up popped the *Sardinian warbler.*

In interviews, Roger explained that one of the high points in his birding experience was the sighting of a *lammergeier* flying overhead clutching lamb bones. The *lammergeier,* also known as the *bearded vulture* because of the black mustache on a buff-yellow head, lives and breeds on crags in high mountainous regions. It subsists mostly on bone marrow and has learned to carry bones to a height and drop them onto rocks below, smashing them into smaller pieces. I was with him that day; we were jostled in the back of a stake truck, hanging on for dear life while riding perilously on a narrow road close to the mountain's edge on our way to Zeus' Cave, when the famed *lammergeier,* bearing a lamb bone, slowly soared overhead. I, too, will never forget that moment.

My third memory of RTP comes from Roger's debarking from a birding tour boat onto the shore of Garden Key in the Dry Tortugas, where my husband and I were camping. Upon seeing Bill, he rushed up and asked, "Do you have a boat?" They happily paddled in our rubber raft over to Bush Key to photograph the nesting *brown noddies* and *noddy terns*—until a motorized skiff approached the oblivious pair and suggested that Roger return to the main group. After all, the passengers had paid to go birding with RTP.

My last picture of Roger Tory Peterson is from when my husband purchased an embroidered blue cotton shirt at a tourist's sidewalk stall. Roger liked it so much he bought its mate. I have the photograph to prove it: two big men dressed as if they were twins, grinning at me.

These are my memories of an often forgetful but outstanding personality of our age. I was lucky to have spent time with him, a man with such dedication to his passion that the world acknowledges him among the greats: RTP.

NICE PEOPLE: THE COOK
May 1988

The air was clear and sparkling over the mountains of west China as my three companions and I emerged from the windowless and doorless remnant of a small cement structure that had formerly housed the Wolong panda research team.

Several days ago we had climbed up from the last village after our drive from Chengdu, the capital of Sichuan Province in China. We had picked our way, carefully, with the help of mini-flashlights, through three long mountain tunnels as we stumbled over the wet, rock-strewn floors. Village men had been hired to carry our backpacks, and several times it was necessary to rest. I winced inwardly at the betrayal of my strong personal convictions against smoking, but, knowing that an American cigarette was more valuable than a gold nugget, it was here that I offered the pack of cigarettes I had brought for such an occasion. The ruddy-faced luggage-bearers sat on the cliff's edge and smoked and smiled.

After the last tunnel, we emerged into the brilliant sunshine of a May afternoon. We quickened our steps along the last climb to the station, where we stashed our gear in the small bedrooms, unrolled sleeping bags onto thin, straw-filled mattresses, and burst outside to begin our search for the birds that make their homes at this high altitude.

Though the days were comfortably cool, constantly we hiked and climbed until my hair, under the necessary sun hat, became damp with perspiration. Rarely were we in the camp area at midday. I looked up at the sky. The sun blazed. And rushing down the mountain, channeled through a wooden chute, flowed a continuous steam of cold, bubbling water. I made a sudden decision to wash my hair. I darted back into our lodging for shampoo and a towel, and, to the astonishment of my companions, let the icy water shoot onto my head. I happily scrubbed away the grime that had accumulated during our outdoor sojourn.

Then, as I bent down to rinse away the soap, a little man emerged from behind the blanket we had hung as a door. It was our Chinese cook. He carried two big bowls, one filled with hot water. He had a plan. He mixed the waters to a comfortable warm temperature and gently poured cupfuls over my locks until the suds disappeared. I toweled my hair until almost dry and would let the warmth of the sun do the rest.

I don't remember the name of the cook, but he stood beside me, obviously pleased with himself. At that moment I realized that our small group of three birders and our leader, Ben King, with a staff of two drivers, two cooks, and a young girl interpreter, had become a family. As we passed through villages, our cooks had purchased fresh greens. They began their day before dawn, chopping the vegetables for the ten-course meals that appeared on our table for breakfasts and dinners. I still don't understand why soup was always served last. The drivers chuckled at my efforts until, from the many selections on the big round table (food was never passed around), I successfully reached for the offerings with chopsticks. At the evening meal, every night one of the men offered me a can of Chinese beer, smiling, as he knew I would drink only half of it. I loved our mountain life.

We repacked to leave for the higher elevations of Tibet. Yes, we were a family setting out on a holiday. And I will always remember the gentle, smiling face of the little cook—what a Nice Person!

REE NANCARROW
1973

Prowling around outside someone's empty house really gives one a queer feeling. We had put ourselves in that compromising position while trying to find the home of Ree Nancarrow, prize-winning Alaskan artist, after asking directions at Denali National Park headquarters. In Alaska everybody seems to know everybody else, so here we were, five miles from the park entrance, hoping we had found the right place.

A photograph of one of Ree's silk-screened prints of the *common loon* in a copy of *Alaska* magazine had caught our eye, and we wanted to purchase one. Nobody home: bad luck.

The dark log cabin almost touched the edge of the water. The blue-green pond, framed by cross-hatched fallen trees and bushes, accentuated the deep green of the nearby forest densely packed with spike-tipped spruce trees. Late-afternoon gray clouds scudded across the Alaskan sky. We wandered around the rustic dwelling and the adjacent pond, hoping to discover signs of life, but only a pair of unwary *pintails* floated into view.

We drove our station wagon, filled with camping gear, toward the spectacular mountains. We forgot about Ree when we entered the wild and rugged vastness of the national park. Graveled riverbeds, evergreen forests, grizzly bears, and caribou surprised us at every turn. A *golden eagle* soared in the sky overhead and a *gyrfalcon* swooped by. We passed all the campgrounds, even Wonder Lake on the far side, and established ourselves at private Camp Denali. From there we explored the wilderness, where we encountered *hawk owls, arctic warblers, ptarmigan, wheatears,* and wild blueberries. We panned for gold.

An early and unexpected August snowstorm locked us away from the outside world until snowplows could clear the gap at Ileson Center. Three days later we were the first travelers to make the ninety-mile traverse over slippery roads, where, in the absence of human activity, the wild animals grazed close by, bear cubs chased one another, and rock ptarmigan pecked at snow-dusted bushes along the edge of the road.

We remembered Ree when we were again driving near her home on our afternoon departure from the park. Impulsively we turned into her driveway, and before we could knock on the door of the cabin, a smiling face appeared at the kitchen window. It was indeed the young artist, who, with her husband and two small sons, had chosen to tuck herself away in this often inhospitable land where for half of each year the sun scarcely shines, winter days grow dark too soon, and deep snow locks out the world.

We asked if we could buy a print of the *loon.* She said she was sorry but they had all been sold. She invited us to come in and look at some more recent works.

The unprecedented early snow had sifted down into the trees and brush that encircled the pond, which merged with the living room, in its close proximity under an enormous picture window, into a beautiful wildlife scene. The aroma of freshly baked bread and cookies came from the kitchen, which was decorated with a collection of primitive tools of the housewife's profession. Ree's mother, who was visiting from her home in Minnesota, sat knitting in a wooden rocking chair.

Ree, on a summer vacation from the University of Minnesota, had worked at Camp Denali and met her future husband there, and had returned to make Alaska her home. He was a carpenter. Ree pointed with pride to the boys' room he had designed with play-sleeping quarters, an indoor jungle gym constructed of wooden planks, for them to climb about on during the confining winter days.

Ree led us to her upstairs studio. There she demonstrated the silk-screening process and showed us the frames where she superimposed color upon color according to her painstakingly detailed patterns. Her tremendous creative talent also stirred her to explore other fields—at the moment, spinning and weaving. I, too, am a spinner and weaver. This was exciting.

We had already chosen a pinecone print and a *white-crowned sparrow* print when we discovered the *pintail*! Only a few were off the screen. Ree scanned a fresh print, discarded it, cast aside several others, and finally found one that satisfied her high standards and signed it.

We were invited to stay for tea and the still-warm-from-the-oven cookies. Suddenly we realized that the afternoon hours had flown by. Ree's gift for reaching into the depths of her spirit to gladden the world around her sent us off into the fading day warm and inwardly glowing.

So we stored away the memory of an unexpected Alaskan friendship. Later that year we read in *Alaska* magazine that Ree Nancarrow had won prizes in an all-Alaska art competition and would soon present a one-person show in Anchorage. We recalled the family's preparation for the long, dark wintertime. But we knew there could be no lack of sunshine with Ree in the house. And Ree still reaches out to us in the lovely *pintail* print, which, since our return from our Alaska summer, has hung in a place of honor above the fireplace in our living room. It is one of our proudest possessions.

A WOODLAND SYMPHONY
1956

After a day's drive from Acadia National Park, our family, consisting of my husband and four children and me, pulling a camping trailer behind our station wagon, in early evening entered the campground at Baxter State Park in northern Maine.

Dinner by an open fire, utensils cleaned and stored, a chance to rest when I heard organ music emanating from the adjacent woods. Astonished, my husband and I, hand in hand, slowly moved toward the enchanting sounds. As we reached the edge of the woodland, suddenly I realized that we were listening to the evensong of thrushes.

The ascending tremolo of the *Swainson's thrush* mingled with the descending notes of the *veery*; the bubbly liquid song of the *wood thrush*; and the clear, flute-like trill of the *hermit thrush*. The sounds blended into a symphonic poem that spiraled into the air and sought out the corners of their forest home.

We lingered until the never-to-be-forgotten concert died away. Then, reverently, we retraced our steps in the night's stillness. We call such encounters "life's bonuses": the unexpected, extra-special experiences that make our spirits soar.

HAPPY LANDINGS

My first breathtaking, heart-fluttering airplane descent
came on a flight from Nome, Alaska, to the Inuit village of Gambell on St. Lawrence Island in the Bering
Sea. There was no guarantee that we would be able to land on
this often cloud-and-fog-shrouded island, but our pilot, Otis,
an experienced Arctic flier, discovered a hole in the cloud bank,
dove into it, and landed on a gravel bar between the ocean and
a large inland lake. Later we learned how the weather in that
region affects flying conditions when our planned four-day stay
stretched into a week, until Otis, careering in on a twenty-knot
wind, under a three-hundred-foot cloud ceiling, could finally land
and pick us up for our return to the mainland.

The flight to the fishing camp at Junglaven, south of the
Orinoco River in Venezuela, was a different matter. Our little
plane buzzed down onto a strip of grass outlined with pop
cans. No night landings here! Upon leaving camp, after traveling the three-mile stretch of narrow dirt track, at one end
of the grass runway a weather-beaten wooden bench offered

respite while I waited for a flight without a timetable.

The four main islands in the Fiji archipelago were served only by small planes. Sunflower Air seemed a perfect name for transport that, except for the international airport at Nadi, always landed on grass. Every time we took off or landed, our lightweight aircraft, which sometimes felt as if it had been constructed of cardboard, fluttered like a butterfly. The number of passengers allowed to fly was determined by the weight of the luggage and items, carried by a mail service, to small stores on the islands. The only security check was a mark the pilot made opposite my name on the manifest.

The float plane that carried us from Key West, Florida, on our many ninety-mile flights to Bush Key in the Dry Tortugas, did not encounter stormy weather. But after surveying the broad expanse of ocean dotted with dark green islands below, the sudden approach to land, on which a huge brick structure had been built during the Civil War years, ended with a smashing contact with ocean waves. So I never felt really safe until we taxied toward the sandy beach and I jumped into the shallow water and waded onto dry land.

Flying in a small plane from Namibia into Botswana in Africa was the established method of connecting the fishing camps and tourist lodges. Our pilot flew as low over the Okavango Delta as he dared so that we might spot the rare antelope, which we did—several of them. Nearing the Chobe camp, we looked down in vain for a landing strip. We saw only herds of grazing zebra and Thompson's gazelles, until a Land Rover appeared, which scattered the animals as it raced around the field, and we landed safely in the now-cleared grassy area.

Probably the most scenic of our daunting flights was our trip with Jerry Stensel, a freelance pilot out of Kotzebue, Alaska, into Gates of the Arctic National Park. My husband and I were tightly jammed into the small space between our pilot and the tail of the Piper Cub. At the edge of the Brooks Range, the wing of Jerry's little plane almost clipped the stone face of the mountain as he flew close enough to show us the *gyrfalcon* nest tucked into a cliff. As we descended and landed on an expanse of sand, no habitation was in sight. We followed Jerry through an opening into the woods and found three tents and a fire pit, the campsite completely hidden in a grove of trees along the Susitna River. A few days later, on our way out, Jerry landed his Piper Cub on a sloping mountain meadow in order to show us his log cabin hideaway. With knees to chest, I sat in the afternoon sunshine among the delicate mountain flowers that blanketed the mountainside as far as the eye could see.

I still remember, as a child, watching a tiny, single-wing Piper Cub land in a field encircled by a barbed-wire fence, near my hometown on the North Dakota prairie. This was a great event in our little community. It was our first view of the wonder of wonders, the feat of flying that we had only heard or read about.

During my lifetime I have traveled over huge distances in ever larger fossil-fueled jet aircraft, but my recollections of the offbeat, often nearly impossible landings in out-of-the way corners of the world are my favorites. Each time I climbed out over the frail fuselage and dropped back onto the comforting solid earth, I whispered softly to myself, "Thank you for a happy landing."

BIRDER'S DICTIONARY

pelagic

You are at a dinner party and you see your good birding buddy on the opposite side of the table. You lean over and say, "Hey, I flew into Monterey last weekend and went on one of Debbie's pelagics. Got an *ashy storm petrel*." The other diners look agape.

You assume that they all know that Monterey is in California. But only a birder worth his salt would know that Debbie is Debbie Shearwater, who on weekends runs a boat out into Monterey Bay to search for ocean birds, otherwise known as pelagics.

The ocean shelf is close to shore there, so it doesn't take all day to reach deep water. Take a lunch and sunscreen, and if you have a tendency to seasickness, be sure to fill your pockets with salty crackers. Other well-known pelagic hotspots are San Diego, California; Westport, Washington; Baltimore, Maryland; and Cape Hatteras, North Carolina.

Personally, among non-birders, I do not think this appropriate dinner table conversation. You just couldn't wait to share your good luck.

pish

You are walking along a forest trail and hear a bird call. You stand impatiently, wait a few minutes, lean down, and stretch on tiptoe, but you cannot see the bird. Finally, in exasperation, you say, *"Pish, pish."* The bird might think that it is a baby bird in distress, or a snake, or some other enemy and pop out to see what is going on. Of course, when he sees you, he disappears. But you have had a good look. *Catbirds, cardinals, song sparrows,* and *yellow warblers* are particularly susceptible to this ruse, but anything might turn up. It's worth a try. Some people frown on pishing, but if evolution means change, I think pishing will only make birds even smarter than they already are.

midden

Any birder who has spent time on St. Lawrence Island in the Bering Sea knows that middens are the best places to look for rare birds that have flown off course and need hiding places. Middens are shallow excavations, hollowed out by Inuit women and children during the few summer months when the permafrost melts just enough so they are able to dig into it.

Former Arctic peoples lived mostly underground, their shelters supported by whale bones, so housekeeping tools, hunting tools, and carved artifacts are much valued by museum collectors. I once saw the curator from a museum in Anchorage write a check for one hundred and fifty dollars to a woman who offered a harpoon with a beautifully carved handle. Money is not easy to come by on that isolated island, so the digging continues.

My friend Beda one day climbed into her attic and returned with gifts of a carved wooden bowl, a needle made from walrus tusk, and a length of braided thread made from seal sinew. I knew how precious that collection was, but also that it would break Beda's heart if I did not accept it.

My husband made the first photo of a *stonechat* in North America, which was found in the midden nearest the village of Gambell on St. Lawrence Island, and it was published in *American Birds*. And one early morning as I trudged through the midden, I discovered an *Oriental pratincole* crouched on the edge of a crevasse. While my husband ran to find the guide Jon Dunn and his group of birders who were on the beach hoping to see an *ivory gull*, I became google-eyed from staring at the little bird, hoping it would not fly away before the others arrived. This will give you some idea of what might turn up in a midden.

o'clock

"Two o'clock" might not be clear to a bystander in the woods at ten o'clock in the morning, but a birder would instantly know where to look for a perched bird. If there is anything that makes a bird mad, it is someone waving arms and pointing at him. So experienced birders stand very still and announce something like, "Straight ahead, the middle acacia tree, two o'clock," and there sits a *wood-pewee* waiting for his dinner to fly by. Or a birder might say, "Look at twelve o'clock on the tallest pine tree for the *pine grosbeak*." On the other hand, if it was a *warbler*, it could be anywhere by now.

kettle

Did you ever look up on a windy spring day and see a mass of tightly packed mosquito-like clouds slowly working its way north? At first you see just a dark blob, and then you spot individuals and they turn out to be birds, milling about, swirling in unison, effortlessly borne by the air beneath them. This is called a kettle. Most of the kettles I have seen are *broadwing hawks* with their black-and-white-banded tails spread out like fans, or *brown-necklaced Swainson's hawks.* You've heard of a "kettle of fish." Now you've heard of a "kettle of birds." You are learning.

patch

According to Webster's dictionary, a patch can be a piece of material applied to cover or mend a hole or tear, a dressing applied to a wound, a small plot of ground, a scrap of any material, or a small piece of greased leather used in ramming home a rifle ball.

To a birder, a patch is a means of identification. "White patch" occurs more than any other descriptive term in a field guide. It begins with the *American wigeon,* which is identified in flight by a large white wing patch on the upperwings. A *mockingbird* has white wing patches that flash when he flies. There are many more, but these are good examples.

Some birds have a black patch; for example, the bold black belly patch of a *dunlin* in breeding plumage, and the black ear patch of the little *olive warbler.* A yellow patch is quite popular too. Everyone recognizes the yellow shoulder patch of a *goldfinch.* There are more colorful patches too: the chestnut, orange, and green of *orioles* and *warblers,* and, in flight, the buffy wing patch of the *short-eared owl.*

So I suggest that Mr. Webster add another category to his patch list: "birdpatch: feathers of any color, found on any part of the body of a bird to aid in identification on the ground or in the air." New words are added to the English vocabulary every year, and this is my nomination.

least

How would you like to be called a "least one"? The worthless, no-account good-for-nothing. Maybe that is why the *least flycatcher* crouches on a limb under a dark leaf in the forest, or the *least grebe* hides in the tall grasses at the edge of the pond.

A notch above, the "lessers" don't mind showing their bright feathers, especially the *lesser goldfinch* gathering dead dandelion froth for its nest, or the long-legged *lesser yellowlegs* marching about knee-deep in water near shore.

Being "little" isn't so bad either. How about the *little blue heron* quietly stalkin the shore's edge? Maybe the *pygmy nuthatch* fits in here.

Being "common" puts you right in the middle of the pack. Because there are so many of you, you really are common. Loons, ducks, hawks, warblers, sparrows—there are just too many to describe.

"Greats" are usually fairly large, as the *great black-backed gull,* which has a thirty-inch wingspan. Or the *great crested flycatcher,* whose *"wheep"* is the only call I've ever been able to imitate and get a bird to respond.

In the *rail* family, the "king" is the winner.

But the shocker is "magnificent," as the *magnificent frigatebird* has the longest wingspan in relation to body weight, and the *magnificent hummingbird* is only five and a half inches long but so fierce that it will drive other hummingbirds away from feeding stations.

I guess being "least" isn't so bad after all.

Now I am a great-grandmother, so you could say "old," "elder," "eldest." Or you could say, "It's *great* to be alive!"

THE WILD WINGS INTERNATIONAL BEAUTY CONTEST

I have seen one hundred and seventy-five hummingbird species in the world, of which twenty species dwell in our own United States, and some are pretty flashy.

To Audubon, a hummingbird is "a glittering fragment of the rainbow—a lovely little creature moving on humming winglets through the air, suspended as if by magic in it, flitting from one flower to another, with motions as graceful as they are light and airy, pursuing its course and yielding new delights whenever it is seen."

But how does one describe a bird that darts in and out of sight like streaks of a rainbow? Can one hummingbird be more beautiful than any of the others? I decided to hold a beauty contest.

First I consulted the field guides for clues to enable me to better judge this parade of contestants. The names of some birds are self-descriptive. For example: *woodcreeper, treehunter, foliage gleaner, fruiteater, flower-piercer, fire-wood-gatherer,* and, yes, even *woodpecker,* and most are plain gray or brown and scurry around doing their little jobs as described. As you will see, humming-bird names have a sort of tenor of their own. So here we go.

> Flowers in the canopy
> Tell me who the fairest be.
> Crimson, purple, gold or blue
> Do you have a favorite hue?
> Glittering, bronzy or emerald green,
> Help me, help me, find the Queen.

Let's begin in our closest neighbor to the south.

Mexico

Violet-crowned fairy: This hummingbird has a forehead and crown of flashing violet and immaculate white underparts. Its velvety black mask is bordered by a glittering green malar stripe. How would you like to meet this small creature at a forest edge or in a garden as it gleans insects from outer foliage of trees?

Costa Rica

Over the border we find more colorful contestants.

Blue-throated goldentail: In dry regions or evergreen gallery, look for a bronzy-green bird. As it flits away notice the bright golden-bronze tail. As it sips nectar watch for a red bill with a black tip.

Adorable coquette: Coquettes are tiny and have bushy crest feath-ers, and plumes that spring fan-like from their cheeks. The long, wispy cheek-tufts are glittering green. You'll find it high in the forest canopy, where it gleans tiny insects from mass-flowering trees—that is, if you can catch the quick fluttering at all.

Scintillant: I found this hummingbird by looking down into the crater of the Irazu Volcano, though it likes hedgerows and coffee plantations. You'd recognize this colorful bird by its rufous tail coverts and brilliant orange-red gorget. The *scintillant* is bigger than some and makes conspicuous dive displays to repel invaders.

Violet sabrewing: This hummingbird likes bananas, so you can find it in a banana plantation or at the edges of mountain forests. As its name implies, it has a deep violet body. It is very large and has a long decurved bill, and its favorite flower is heliconia, which is a good thing, as they are plentiful in Central and South America.

Panama

Moving south into Panama, I was surprised that this small country has its own supply of hummingbirds.

Violet-bellied: Not often found around habitation, but common in forest borders, clearings, and bushy slopes, it has a glittering green throat, and its underparts are a dark violet blue. Quite a combination.

Snowcap: The spectacular male is unmistakable. The dark reddish-purple body has a snowy white crown and a mostly white tail. It is uncommon, found only from the Caribbean slope. It is tiny and is a tail-flicker. Good luck.

Venezuela

Let's move down to Venezuela and see what we can find.

Orange-throated sunangel: The upper breast is a glittering golden-orange, below which is a cinnamon-buff breast band. Added to all that color, the central tail feathers are golden-green. But to find one, you will have to move up to cloud or dwarf forest.

Amethyst woodstar: One of the smallest, with wing beats eighty beats a second that create a distinctive buzz. Look in low bushes and small trees for a bird with throat and sides of neck glittering rosy-red and a white band across the breast.

Crimson topaz: This time we have a rain forest bird. The nape and upper back are glittering fiery purple, shading to gold on the tail coverts. The central tail feathers are shining gold-bronze, very long and curved and protruding beyond the rest. The throat is an irisidcent, glittering topaz, the belly an iridescent, glittering crimson.

Green-tailed goldenthroat: Bright emerald-green tail, outer feathers tipped with white. Below, the tail is a glittering golden-green. Its home is the Amazonian forest edge or second-growth scrub. Nice not to have to search so high.

Ecuador

The country of Ecuador is our next stop, working our way south.

Shining sunbeam: Large, cinnamon rufous, an upper montane species found in stunted woodlands and gardens. The crown gradually becomes glittering rosy-violet, and glittering golden-green on rump.

Amethyst-throated sunangel: This tiny creature has a coppery-purple crown and glittering blue frontlet, and the throat is purple with a white pectoral band bordered below by a glittering green band.

Violet-tailed sylph: The gorget spot is glittering violet, and the outermost tail feathers are very long, shining metallic violet with blue tips. It forages from the lowest underbrush to the tallest treetops, so your chances of finding one are good.

Meridian metaltail: This species, with its glittering green throat patch, is uncommon in scattered bushes at tree line in the west Andes. The head and under tail are shining green.

Lazuline sabrewing: This is a combination of glittering green above with its throat and vest a glittering violet-blue. Outer tail coverts are rufous chestnut; it helps to know that the bill is decurved.

Rufous-throated sapphire: Finally, a hummingbird with a bright orange-red bill. It is a dark shining green little bird with a rufous chin and a glittering blue throat and chest. It is found in humid savanna forest or shrubby clearings.

Sapphire-vented puffleg: Look in open grass or bushy slopes, where they alight on the ground to feed on tiny flowers. Glittering violet under tail coverts, a long blue-black tail, and white leg puffs are really cute and a good reason for finding this bird.

Brazil

Brazil is a huge country, so should be home to lots of hummingbirds. We'll see.

Blue-tufted starthroat: Wow! This hummingbird has a glittering violet-red throat. The slightly forked tail is bronze-green. It favors scrub and woodland edges.

Violet-capped woodnymph: The glittering green gorget is in contrast to the glittering violet-blue underparts. The blue-black tail is deeply forked—one of the more unusual characteristics of hummingbirds. It is common in humid or wet forest in the lowlands or foothills.

Tourmaline sunangel: Small, the breast and frontlet are glittering green, while the gorget is glittering violet-blue. Surprise! There is a large rose patch on the throat. It feeds in humid and wet forest borders, shrubby pastures, and hedges.

Spangled coquette: One of the hummingbirds that has a buffy-white band across the rump, an easy field mark when the bird is flying away, which is usually the case. It has bushy crest feathers that cover the sides of its head and neck. This one's a tiny one, uncommon, usually seen in the canopy of tall trees.

Peru

Let's pop over to Peru.

Sapphire-spangled emerald: A lowland hummer, with a broad white line down the center of the belly. The bill is curved and red at the base.

Golden-tailed sapphire: The tail coverts and tail are shining golden-copper, which is probably where it got its name. It has a squeaky two-note song steadily repeated from the canopy of flowering trees.

Sparkling violetear: In parks and gardens as well as semi-open highlands, a more common species that in addition to sipping nectar, hawks insects. Its ear-coverts are sparkling violet-blue. The tail has dark sub-terminal bands.

Bolivia

The next stop on our way south.

Violet-throated starfrontlet: A rufous rump and tail contrast with the bronzy-green body of this hummingbird with a glittering violet patch on the throat and a cinnamon belly. As with others of this genus, it "traplines" low flowers and is often found in flocks.

Violet-fronted brilliant: This bird is solitary, does not gather in groups in flowering trees, and frequently flycatches. The crown is glittering violet. The tail is large and forked.

Jewelthroat: It has a small black chin spot, and across the breast is a bright orange-rufous band. This little hummer is an inconspicuous bird of shady forest understory.

Argentina

And now we are down to our last stop.

Blue-tufted starthroat: The throat is a glittering violet-red, while the underparts and tufts on the sides of the neck are glittering blue. In display, the male drops, then rises in three short steps in front of the female while singing and expanding neck tufts.

Red-tailed comet: At last, an unmistakable bird. Hurrah! It is mainly glossy green, but the long red, black-barred tail is conspicuous. It likes forest and savannas in the Andean hills.

And who is the winner?

First place goes to the *crimson topaz,* followed by the *violet-purple coronet* in second, and the *blue-tufted starthroat* in third.

At the beginning I stated that I would consult field guides, which I have done, and the "glittering," "shining," "brilliant," "flashing," and "sparkling" are all in the texts. How happy I was when I discovered that Crawford Greenewalt, the master photographer of hummingbirds, agrees with me. In his book *Hummingbirds,* he states, "In many ways this is the most gorgeous of the hummingbirds, fully justifying its name, 'the beautiful topaz.'"

I hope my readers will agree that "a thing of beauty is a joy forever."

Even the scientist Sir William Jardine introduces his monograph on hummingbirds, published in 1833, with the following lines:

> His silken vest was purfled o'er with green,
> And crimson rose leaves wrought with sprigs between.
> His diadem, a topaz, beam'd so bright,
> The moon was dazzled with its purest light.

Today I looked out my window and thrilled at the sight of a *ruby-throated* hummingbird at my feeder in Michigan.

I'D RATHER BE HERE
THAN ANYWHERE ELSE ON EARTH

Norway

I am a Viking, as all four of my grandparents emigrated to America from Norway. So I have come to this country to meet the descendants of the sister who remained behind. We quickly become friends with my newfound cousins, and we rent a small apartment in Trondheim, the former capital, and settle in for a summer's stay. Soon we discover that daily coastal ferries sail along the shore, serving the otherwise isolated villages tucked into the fjords. They deliver mail, pick up broken machines and take them in for repairs, and collect the wonderful, huge strawberry crops to be sold in the city. The fjords are deep ocean invasions along the coast where steep peninsulas with high, massive walls extend, like fingers, into the sea. As we sail deep into the Geiranger fjord, from the open deck of the little boat I gaze up at the jagged cliffs and the sparkling waterfalls and into the deep blue ocean. At this special moment, the sun shining and the wind blowing my hair, I feel serene. I belong.

Iceland

My husband, my ten-year-old son, and I were camping in Iceland. After spending a few days with friends in Reykjavik, we flew to the northern village of Akuyreyi, where the volcanic surface of the land is so rough and irregular that the area was used by astronauts as they prepared to land on the moon. Overhangs of small caves protected our nightly campfires. One day it rained, so we boarded a tourist bus to view the geysers, their plumes emanating from the many fissures over the countryside, and to walk among the smoking sulfur pools. At last the bus stopped at the entrance to two hot-water caverns — one for men and one for women. As we entered the cave, already feeling the heat from the accumulated steam, one of the women announced that she had come prepared for this moment by wearing a bathing suit under her traveling clothes. She undressed and lowered herself into the pool. That was too much! My clothing was off in an instant, from down jacket to turtleneck sweater, wool knickers, underwear, everything. Behind me I saw another woman undress and join me, swimming in the gently moving underwater stream. As she swam she murmured, *"Das ist wunderbar! Das ist wunderbar!"* I agreed. *Das war wunderbar!*

Kachemak Bay

Kachemak Bay in Alaska is an undeveloped pristine national park, and I have invaded its forest sanctuary to find, deep at the end of the woodland trail, a scene from time primeval — the remains of a glacial lake, shimmering in the sunshine, surrounded by giant rocks. As a result of a bygone landslide, the broken fragments have haphazardly piled up into a bizarre natural amphitheater.

I climb onto a giant rock and rest from my journey through the northern forest of mixed pines and oaks. I gaze down into the blueness of the peaceful icy lake and am filled with awe at the geological history of our planet that lies before me. I linger knowing that I will not come this way again.

The Tepuis

Tepuis are flat-topped, sheer-walled mountains that extend over a five-hundred-mile area of green savanna and forest in the Guayanan highlands of South America. Strange and spectacular scenery gives them a primeval otherworldly feel. In these "islands in time," one finds flora and fauna that occur nowhere else on earth, and I was on my way to camp there. Indistinct rectangular, flat-topped gray blocks floated like a mirage in the far distance, seemingly forever; but, at last, we arrived at a mountaintop campsite. We erected our lightweight tents, cooked dinner over an open fire, and gratefully sank into our sleeping bags. Sometime after midnight, I awoke. As I slipped out into the utter silence, the night was almost as bright as day. Someone had turned on the moon! It seemed I could almost touch it. Twinkling stars, clustered like chandeliers, hung from the sky. It seemed that the whole world softly blanketed my frail body. Then, in the heavens, I saw my very first Southern Cross. The midnight silence was like a prayer.

A Treetop Sanctuary

Reunion Island is a small island in the Indian Ocean, a French protectorate, its mountains splashed with colorful tropical flowers. Beauty is everywhere. But I am sitting in the topmost branch of a ponderosa pine tree, looking down across the treetops of an impenetrable jungle forest. I have risked my life to climb to this position and am sitting on an unprotected wooden perch that has been attached to the treetop, the final slim tip of the trunk poking up through a hole in the wooden slab. I pull my knees up against my chest and concentrate on finding a rare bird, a *pink pigeon*, which does not come. It is raining a fine mist. I reach into my backpack for a banana and bag of trail mix. As the hours pass I wonder why I am so content up here on my lofty perch. *Aha,* I think to myself. *I am near the clouds and on top of the world.*

The *Professor Khromov*

I have gone to sea on an old Russian ship, the *Professor Khromov,* formerly a Russian oceanographic research vessel, so there are no modern salons, casinos, or swimming pools. The South Atlantic is rough, but the oceanic birds love the strong, high winds. Bundled into down-filled outerwear, as the ship plows into the crashing white-capped waves I have found a sheltered nook on deck. I brace myself against the bulkhead and stand for hours watching the giant *albatrosses* and tiny *petrels* in their swooping and swirling dance against the sunless gray sky. Standing there, I do not tire. Instead, I too feel strong and free.

The Dry Tortugas

The Dry Tortugas are small, waterless tropical islands, ninety miles southwest of Key West, Florida. For many years we have camped there for the first ten days in May. I stroll along the sandy shore, swim in the clear ocean waters, and study the colorful tropical fish from my prone position on the brick moat. I fish for mangrove snapper. I love the little island, which, for the moment, I consider my own. I am the provider, an important person, depended upon. The sunset casts its spell over the evening. From under our tree shelter I recline in my canvas chaise and look out over the vast panorama of blue-green sea and the silhouettes of the surrounding small, dark islands, and I dream.

High in the Sky

I had always wished to go up in a hot air balloon, but I didn't do it until I was eighty-five. I had traveled to many countries as a birder, so this visit to Turkey was my first experience as a tourist. Every day we rambled among the outdoor ruins of ancient cities, and I was the first to sign up excitedly for a balloon flight over the ancient land of Cappadocia. We boarded the giant capsule before sunrise as dawn sent its rosy fingers creeping over the edge of the world. Through the centuries, steep valleys had been etched into the granite mountains, becoming jagged, meandering fissures in the earth's crust. A Grand Canyon! I was suspended in the cool air of the shimmering dawn, above the vast panorama; the emerging daylight cast shadows on the landscape below. As I gently swayed, suspended between heaven and earth, my small person seemed to be a tiny atom in the expanding universe. I was in the present but also a part of the past.

The Green Trail

It was a Sunday morning in October on the Green Trail, a hiking trail close to my home in Michigan. I stopped to look up into the fall maple leaves that Jack Frost had splashed with red and yellow paint. The morning sun filtered down through the softly waving foliage, creating a pattern of lace against a cloudless blue sky. As I lingered, bathed in the day's warm glow, my heart was filled with peace.

I AM A BIRD!
July 2011

This is how it began. The phone rang. The caller was my son, Matt, who usually does not phone during business hours.

"What's up?" I asked.

He answered in an excited voice, "Mom, you are going to get your birthday present early." This is July; my ninety-second birthday is coming up in September.) "We've arranged for you to get a flying lesson. You've always said you wanted to learn to fly."

I'll admit that off and on over the years I had unguardedly announced to my family that my only regret in a lifetime of adventures is that I'd never learned to fly an airplane.

"Where?" I queried, a tremor in my voice.

"At the St. Clair County Airport." A half-hour drive from my home in Fort Gratiot, Michigan. "Julie [my granddaughter] knows a pilot who knows an instructor there. We'll let you know the details." I could tell that Matt was worried I would say no. "This is your birthday. Go for it!"

You could say that this came as a sort of shock, like a dream from which you will awake and find the normal day stretching ahead. "I can't, I can't," I said to myself. Then I remembered my son's pleasure at his great idea, his suppressed excitement when he phoned me with the news, and suddenly I realized this is what I have wanted to do all my life!

A week went by. Then another before an e-mail informed me that my instructor would be Skip Steffens, owner of the plane and the St. Clair Flight Academy. I phoned him. I believe to this day that Skip thought I just wanted to go on an airplane ride. I told him I thought we should talk.

So one evening we met at the airport and, probably to his dismay, I convinced him that I wanted to be the pilot. He sent me home with the biggest book I'd ever seen, *The Airplane Pilot's Training Manual*, and I dug in.

Many years had elapsed since I'd had to study any subject seriously. If I couldn't chase birds from continent to continent, I would *be* a bird. My decision to occupy the pilot's seat in the cabin made it imperative that I understand the basic principles of flying and become familiar with the plane itself.

So I copied the illustrated pages from the text, then covered them with definitions and explanations in red ink. On the backs of those pages, I recorded additional information. I memorized the dials and their functions, and read about how to check oil pressure and how to move the control wheel and the rudder pedals. I learned the importance of attitude, the nose in relation to the horizon.

Skip and I met again. After an inspection of the exterior parts of the plane, I climbed into the cockpit, where I could manipulate the controls—that is, after we piled three cushions under me and I still had to stretch to see the fuselage.

Every day I reviewed my red-inked pages. While driving around town I could be seen mumbling, "Alpha, Bravo, Charlie, Delta, Echo . . ." or "Niner." I planned to be ready.

The sun thrust its first glow of the day into my bedroom at six o'clock. It was Saturday, the day I had been waiting for. Julie, who was to ride with me, was still sleeping on the hide-a-bed in the living room. I tiptoed around to get coffee and cereal, which I took onto my balcony; I saw that it was going to be beautiful, wind-free morning. I crouched over my homemade manual for a frantic last-minute review—the notes I had studied for the past three weeks.

Then we arrived at the little airport and were surrounded by family members: my son Matt and daughter-in-law Patty; my granddaughter Julie; my daughter Laurel, from Wisconsin, and her grandson Ben, from Indiana; my granddaughter Katherine, from New York; and an old friend and neighbor who had somehow heard about what I'd thought was a secret.

I met my copilot, Jerry Kennie, and we were off for a pre-flight inspection—pages and pages of lists, and we checked every one. I helped drain fuel from spouts under the wings into a clear glass to inspect for water or other contamination. I followed Jerry as he pointed out each feature—so important to safe flying.

Julie climbed up first; then, at the last minute, Katherine decided that she wanted to go along and hastily climbed in after her. Time to go. This time I had brought a plump beach cushion, and Skip came up with a wonderfully high cushion with a padded backrest. Almost perfect—but not quite. I called out, "One more pillow!" This was placed at the bottom of the pile. Good job. I could easily reach the rudder pedals and brakes. Seat belts fastened. Windows closed. Call out: "All clear?"

From the moment I pressed on the rudder pedals as I taxied close to the yellow center line in front of me, I felt at home in the little plane. Then we were airborne, pressing the throttle to gain altitude, and Jerry said, "You are in control."

At two thousand feet, keeping the nose of the plane at a proper distance from the horizon came naturally. I banked and turned left, returned to a horizontal position, banked and turned right, and we were flying straight again. I followed the coastline of Lake Huron until we neared the Blue Water Bridge, and my passengers were able to take photos. We joked about flying under the bridge. I was loving it. A surge of happiness swept over me, and I said to myself, "I'd rather be here than anywhere else in the world." I was a bird!

Then it was time to turn west, then north and circle back toward the airport below. I knew we could not put the flaps down until our speed was within the white arc on the airspeed indicator. Then Jerry took over, skimmed close to the surface of the tarmac, and we landed.

I put my left foot on the strut and made the long jump to the ground. My paparazzi rushed toward me. Shouts of congratulations. Cameras. And Skip with a grin from ear to ear. He looked at me and said, "You made my day." And that was the best ending to this day that I could have asked for.

Will I be a bird again? Maybe. Someday.